A Dream Deferred

Guyana, Identities under the Colonial Shadow

Stephen Spencer

First published 2007 in Great Britain
by Hansib Publications Limited
London and Hertfordshire, UK

Email: info@hansib-books.com Website: www.hansib-books.com

ISBN 1 870518 77 2

Cover design by Stefan Brazzo

Design and production by Print Resources, Hertfordshire, England

Printed and bound in Great Britain
by Alden Group Limited

This book is dedicated to Ernestine and Balchand Basdeo

What happens to a dream deferred?
Does it dry up
Like a raisin in the sun?
Or fester like a sore--
And then run?
Does it stink like rotten meat?
Or crust and sugar over--
like a syrupy sweet?
Maybe it just sags
like a heavy load.
Or does it explode?

Langston Hughes
(1902-1967)

CONTENTS

LIST OF ILLUSTRATIONS AND TABLES

ACKNOWLEDGEMENTS

I am indebted to the following people in Trinidad and Guyana for their guidance and hospitality: Ralph Premdas at the University of the West Indies, Dr Dennis Bassier at the University of Guyana, Eusi Kwayana and Dr Rupert Roopnaraine (of the Working People's Alliance) Dr Cheddi Jagan (who passed away in 1996) and Arnold Apple (writer and political observer).

Thanks also to Dr Gary Taylor who saw the potential for a readable text in a much less readable thesis.

Stephen Spencer.
May 2006.
40th Anniversary of Guyana's Independence.

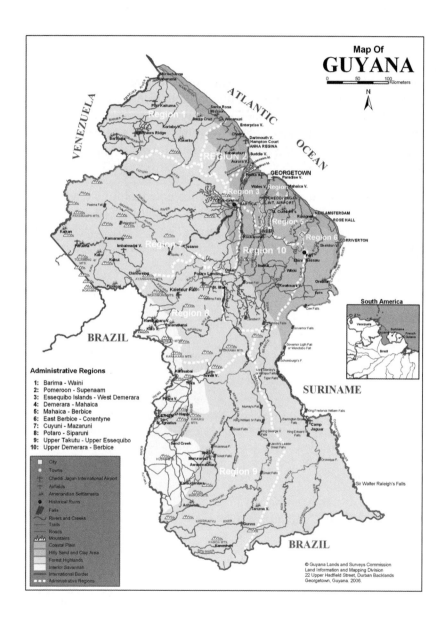

INTRODUCTION

This book is about the processes which have shaped ethnic identity in Guyana, a small English speaking nation on the Caribbean coast of South America.

Guyana had been shaped by the ruthless self interest of four centuries of colonialism. After independence it was another post colonial republic which faded from memory in the west. The people of what was British Guiana demonstrated determination to forge their own destiny and elected Cheddi Jagan and the multi-ethnic People's Progressive Party . While in power from 1957 to 1964 the party, under Dr Jagan, was subjected to severe pressure from Britain seeking to maintain a hold over the country's sugar and mineral wealth, and the USA motivated by cold war anxieties. Foreign intervention, and a desire to see Guyana reach independence under a leader favourable to the western powers, generated an acrimonious struggle dividing the nation along racial lines, before independence was finally granted from Britain in 1966. This divide has had a devastating impact on Guyana's political, social and economic well being.

Yet some older Guyanese have a memory of a country with abundant promise; one of the best educated countries in the Caribbean and also one of relative affluence. Guyana has produced a great many talented writers, artists, sportsmen and women, musicians, and political leaders. Many Guyanese feel that a very bright future was snatched away from them on the eve of the country's hard fought for independence, and dreams of a destiny being fulfilled were dashed. Guyana is now one of the poorest countries in the Western hemisphere, and one with a seemingly intractable pattern of ethnic polarisation. This book sets out to explore the nature of this divide and the complex relationships between culture, social and political history and ethnic identity in Guyana.

Guyana's Ethnic Mix

Guyana, a country situated on the north east shoulder of South America, is bound on the west by Venezuela, on the east by Surinam, and to the south by Brazil. The country, however, is historically a functional part of the Caribbean, and as a result of two centuries of colonialism has a multi-ethnic population dominated by Indians and Africans.

The population of Guyana is comprised of six ethnic groups. Estimates vary but the relative size of these populations are: African (36-40%), East Indian (51%), Chinese (0.6-2%), Portuguese (1.3%), Amerindian (4-7%), and Mixed (7-13%) The population of Guyana is estimated to be between 765,000 to 825,000.[1]

Mainstream religion is broken down into Christian (40%), Hindu (35%), Muslim (9%). Although reliable data was not available, conservative estimates of Guyanese living in other countries (especially US, Canada and UK) could be close to 700,000 (around the indigenous population of Guyana). The US Census Bureau (2000) estimated 200,000 Guyanese across the USA alone.[2]

Almost all of the population is concentrated on a 5 to 10 mile coastal strip along the country's Atlantic coast. The majority of Indians live in the rural areas, while the Africans live mainly in the towns; Georgetown, the capital, is a mainly African-Guyanese town. However, it is not the case that these two groups are rigidly segregated from one another. Nevertheless, patterns of segregation do exist, and these are a legacy of historical factors. The Africans, for example, are concentrated in the towns and villages due to their wish to move away from the plantation system, a system that had brutally exploited them for centuries.

After the emancipation in 1838, the freed slaves built hundreds of houses and asserted their independence.. At this time, mass transportation of Indian indentured labourers began. The Indians, following the Portuguese, '...came last to toil on the estates in Guyana, have been, and continue to be, the backbone of the sugar industry.'[3] Broad distinctions between the two groups can also be drawn in terms of occupational differences, with the Africans being better represented in the civil service, armed forces, police and the trades and professions; whereas the Indians, although their profile in the public sector and the professions seems to be expanding, still dominate agriculture, especially sugar and rice production.

The ethnically heterogeneous population is loosely integrated by a Creole culture that has evolved during the last two hundred and fifty years of Guyanese history. Nonetheless '...strong social integrative institutions are few; they are rivalled by equally strong subcultural patterns that threaten periodically to burst the society asunder at its ethnic seams.'[4] Premdas succinctly captures the plight of Guyana. There is, apart from the pattern of differences so far described, a degree of commonality and integration and thoroughly mixed villages are not unusual. Yet it is a fragile association which from time to time can explode, often due to political manipulation.

US and British Intervention in Guyana's Politics

From the late 1950s up to the present time the political tension between the Africans and Indians intensified. With the gradual withdrawal of the British and the struggle for independence, the two groups were briefly united. But in the post-colonial period, internal and external influences have pushed the groups apart. The colonial powers and the USA viewed the burgeoning radicalism of the first Guyanese political party the PPP, (People's Progressive Party) led by the Cheddi Jagan and Forbes Burnham with growing alarm. The British were alarmed because of their substantial investments, especially in sugar and rum making. The US was also hostile to the new regime because of the intensity of cold war feeling at the time. Jagan's uncompromising Marxist views did not endear him to the Kennedy administration, disturbed at the prospect of another Cuba in its backyard.

These powers intervened. The result, as we shall see, has been a country divided. Old wounds between Africans and Indians were re-opened. The PPP had won a resounding victory in the first election held under universal suffrage in 1953. But the British Governor suspended the constitution after the Jagan government had been in office for only one hundred and thirty three days. Forbes Burnham, an ambitious African, eventually assumed power in 1964, being more acceptable to the foreign powers. In the years after the suspension of the constitution, Burnham had begun to split away from the PPP and align himself with a pro-African movement which formed into the PNC (The People's National Congress). The PNC, under Burnham's leadership, took a more moderate line publicly on political and economic matters and for this reason was considered a much better prospect than Jagan to lead the country into independence. But, under his leadership, independence meant that the new state was dominated by African-Guyanese elites and attended to their interests at the expense of the Indian-Guyanese segment of the population.

After these formative events in the sixties marked by intense inter-ethnic violence, a state of mutual hostility has lingered and deepened. For the most part, this has taken place under the veil of apparent public harmony.

Guyana's Bipolar Ethnic Division

In Guyana, two roughly equal segments face one another across a great social, historical and ethnic divide. Trinidad (a close neighbour of Guyana) Fiji, Malaysia, Canada and others are considered to have similar divisions between ethnic groups. In Guyana there exists considerable institutionalised inequity in the distribution of power between the two ethnic communities. The pro-African People's National Congress achieved dominance politically from 1964 to 1992 using blatant vote rigging and coercion to maintain their position as the ruling elite. In 1992, Jagan; the elder statesman, who had been waiting in the wings for 28 years finally returned to power.

However the bitter power struggle is still prevalent. After the 1997 elections (Janet Jagan and the PPP won a 55% majority) the PNC disputed the results and there were some violent public demonstrations between Indian and African political groups.

In the last decade this has been a regular pattern, and has recently been exacerbated by the outbreak of execution-style killings, which are claimed, by some, to be manifestations of deep racial hatred fostered by those in power on either side of the ethnic divide. However, these killings are thought by other commentators to be less a sign of the operation of ethnic cabals dedicated to ethnic cleansing, than a slide into vicious gang warfare fuelled by the lucrative drug trade. Alleged gangs like the Taliban or Phantom gangs indulge in retaliatory turf wars. While this seems to present a more rational explanation, it is indicative of the ingrained sensitivity that conspiracy theories take root so easily based on the flimsiest of evidence. (see discussion of Kean Gibson's claims p. 23-4, 79-80)

Firstly, however, I will look at the sociological, political and cultural formation of conflict in Guyana's turbulent history.

NOTES AND REFERENCES

1 Figures derived from several sources including: Jan Lahmeyer "populstat" site: 1999/2004, GE Source and the CIA World Fact Book, http://www.cia.gov/cia/publications/factbook/geos/gy.html#P
2 see Orozco, M, 2002
3 M, Gopal, 1992: 17.
4 Premdas, R, 1986: 161.

CHAPTER 1
Explanations for Ethnic Conflict

These constant and deep-seated conflicts seem to stem from long standing enmity, lack of genuine communication between the ethnic blocs, and may be viewed as a manifestation of a long historical process of ethnic boundary construction rather than a recent post-colonial eruption of primordial ethnic difference as claimed by some academics. Indeed, '... ethnic boundaries are constructed from the interaction between groups with shared historical experiences and cultural values and their social environment'.[1] Ethnicity is socially constructed and subject to constant re-evaluation. It may well be that the conflict helps to shape and affirm identity on both sides.

Such boundaries may be strengthened, modified, adapted to deal with new phenomena, or deconstructed as new relationships flourish. This process of social construction clearly operates at all levels in a society, defining social meanings, identity and relationships through shared codes, institutions and practices. In a plural society such as Guyana, each ethnic group maintains both a public and a private face. Turpin maintains that in such societies social action can be understood only by distinguishing between private and public ethnicity. This important distinction is elaborated by Turpin, who argues that, '...social action in the private domain is influenced most significantly by cultural traditions and ideas, and that action in the public domain while drawing on these ideas, is most significantly influenced by class and power relationships.'[2] This acknowledges the importance of social class structures and power relationships, and instead of becoming engaged in a possibly futile debate about the relative prominence of class over race or ethnicity (or vice versa), treats these categories as tools in the examination of different domains and aspects of practice. Furthermore, it avoids the danger of treating ethnicity as monolithic, allowing theoretical space for functionally different types of ethnicity.

Marxist theorists and their critics

The literature on ethnic relations in the Caribbean, and specifically Guyana and Trinidad, has frequently evoked the class versus race debate to describe inter-ethnic differences between Indians and Africans. R.T. Smith, in a pioneering study, observed that, '...a very elaborate system of perception of ethnic differences does exist in Guyanese society, and what makes it particularly complex is the way in which criteria other than physical appearance enter into the process of social identification.'[3] Writing prior to independence, Smith seemed to believe boundaries based on ethnic differences less important than those differences specifically derived from class. Of the African-Guyanese, Smith comments that there, '...has been so much intermixture of Negroes with other races that the ethnic boundaries are often difficult to define and such African culture as survives is very marginal to the everyday life of Guyanese Negroes.'[4] However, Smith does hint at the power of the colonial hegemony. He was aware that Negroes strove towards 'whiteness' in word and deed and tended to look down on Indians.

Traditional Marxist viewpoints see ethnicity as part of a superstructure, and hence flowing from the economic base, and relations of production in a society. R.T. Smith is rather dismissive of ethnic differences, calling them, '...the residue of cultural peculiarities.'[5] Moreover, he stresses that should the source of inequality be removed and equality of opportunity be restored, any ethnic difference would dissolve. Indeed Smith ventures to suggest that the Guyanese are remarkably united by what he vaguely refers to as their 'common cultural equipment.'[6] However, it soon becomes apparent that to create a dichotomy between class and ethnicity, and award clear primacy to the former, misses the complex historical interweaving of processes of class and ethnic formation. Certain differences in ethnicity are frequently channelled, amplified and strengthened through political allegiances. Such was the case in the sequence of events which unfolded in Guyana from the 1960s onwards. Smith also clearly recognised the role of colonial authorities, and in particular noted the influence of US and British governments in actively seeding ethnic division in Guyana.

The suggestion that ethnicity simply lies dormant, to be utilised as the most visible rationale or expression of deeper divisions, inherent in economic structures and the state, is not wholly convincing. Certainly there are class distinctions, but these do not correspond simply with those of ethnic background. Why should ethnic boundaries persist when such boundaries do not correspond to the boundaries defining class interest groups? It is unnecessary for class and ethnicity to be seen as discrete independent variables in a competition for primacy. Rather, it may be possible for both to be viewed as interacting elements in a systematic theory of boundary formation in a society. As Rex (1986) suggests, '...it is not necessary to exclude from consideration the possibility of a situation in which either ethnicity or class, or both together operate as the main means of boundary marking.'[7]

Indians in Guyana have been concerned with maintaining Indian culture and resisting wholesale creolisation. The recognition of cultural differences creates stereotypes about the nature and actions of the 'coolie' and the 'blackman.' '...Ethnic conflict occurs in terms of criticisms, ridicule and invidious comparison of these stereotypes.' [8]

Newman and the origins of ethnic supremacy

Newman (1984) ascribes a major role to the legacy of the plantation system, and the formation of the *'Creole bourgeoisie'* dedicated to the status quo. Noting the growing rift between Indian and African working class movements opposed to colonial rule, Newman argues that alliances developed between African workers and the multi-racial middle classes on the one hand, and Indian workers and the rice farmers on the other. These alliances polarised Guyanese society.[9]

The fact that there are two separate communal working class movements may at times of common effort be ignored. Yet Newman's accurate analysis indicates that there is a gradual drawing of communal lines enhanced by occupational and regional patterns, and the legacy of colonial values formative in the development of the Creole bourgeoisie. The view which begins to form, then, highlights the weakness of the doctrine of assimilation, as an almost natural process within an emerging class society.

John LaGuerre usefully sums up the problems of numerous attempts to explain social relations in ethnically plural societies by use of all embracing social class theories. Marxist theory would assume the emergence of one united working class, but in Guyana, as LaGuerre points out, ethnicity divides more than class unites. It is sometimes assumed that a universal ideology such as socialism might serve to straddle the ethnic groups. In contemporary Guyana, the major parties claim to have socialist roots. Both claim to be based on a *'working class,'* both are led by ethnic leadership. There are essentially two working classes in Guyana.[10]

Critique of Marxism

The character of colonial Caribbean society, with its imported peoples, raises serious questions about the Marxist premise that the economic sub-structure of society determines its superstructure, including the state. Walks argues (along with the plural society theorists) that even the concept of a colour-class stratification system in which there is the fusion or combination of racial and status factors, is an inadequate way of explaining the dynamics of this society.[11] Walks goes on to criticise the concept of ethnicity as an invalid focus for analysis if taken in isolation. Walks warns against treating ethnicity as an idealised and objective phenomenon in itself rather than merely one dimension of complex processes of real group formation in ethnically divided societies. Such appeals, to some sort of primordial ethnicity, exclude a range of factors influencing the historical construction of ethnic boundaries. While much of Walks' thesis appears to reaffirm the crucial nature of class and economic base, he warns against the determinism or simplification inherent in some Marxist approaches.

Bourdieu in describing the processes involved in ethnic boundary formation claims that objectivism is flawed and stresses the dangers of observing social events as purely symbolic exchanges. This is as true for primordialist views of ethnicity, as it is for those of some doctrinaire Marxists. In Guyana, it appears that class factors and cultural differences are inseparable elements in the formation of ethnic identity, and are therefore, not accessible to simplistic Marxist analyses which see ethnicity as merely an illusory barrier to be used in the interests of one class or another.

The Pluralist argument

Furnival believed that plural societies are composed of essentially antagonistic ethnic groups prevented from all-out conflict by the coercive force wielded by colonial powers. Without this control there would be anarchy. These ideas have the consequence, whether intended or not, of providing justification for retaining colonial power. It is also clearly a paternalistic view which carries ready-made assumptions about other cultural traditions. M. G. Smith saw Furnival's distinction between plural and homogeneous societies as useful, but elaborated on it theoretically. He defined pluralism in terms of differences in compulsory institutions (e.g. kinship, education, property, economy, recreation etc.) and minority control of inter-sectional relations, in most examples of colonial government. Such plural societies can be characterised in Smith's view as, '...defined by dissensus and pregnant with conflict'.[12] Smith's analysis marked a significant advance in studies of ethnicity as, '...it introduced an anthropological perspective that looked at relations between ethnic groups rather than at relations within an ethnic group'.[13]

Two broad and distinct possibilities emerge from the plural society theorists: first, that asymmetrical power relations between groups will inevitably lead to struggle and division, with the withdrawal of minority control. Second, that ethnic groups may develop integrative bonds, partly as a result of the colonial domination. This latter view stresses that ethnic relations are not necessarily negative; rather they may constitute 'functional systems.' Schermerhorn rejects an either or dichotomy between *'power/conflict'* and *'functional systems'* approaches. He claims that conflict between groups of unequal power, actively engender integrative bonds that have functional characteristics. He gives the example of British invasion of South African tribal lands. The very obvious power/conflict dimension inherent in this act of aggression, he believed, was balanced by the fact that the tribal allies needed British protection from traditional enemies, therefore, providing an example of a 'functional system'. Both conflict and integration should be viewed as part of a single process.[14]

Ethnicity is a set of real and substantive values affecting every area of life at the individual and community level. Such values, it will be considered, are the direct result of the material conditions, and shared experiences of groups in society. Ethnicity then is the accretion of lived experience, and the shared codes of expression of that experience and identity. Ethnic identity permeates all areas of everyday life; it is a habitual and constantly changing set of parameters, which like linguistic structures, are reproduced and mutated largely without the intervention of conscious thought. Similarly, like language and other social codes, the markers of ethnicity both reflect and help to effect changes within the social sphere. Ethnic boundaries, therefore, have an inherent fluidity and defy traditional objectivist approaches to be reified or determined. Cohen has usefully defined ethnic identity as, '...a series of nesting dichotomizations of inclusiveness and exclusiveness'.[15] This allows a form of distinctive feature analysis which grounds ethnicity in everyday practice rather than in abstract conjecture.

Instrumentalist and Primordialist views of ethnic identity

The instrumentalist view of ethnic identity states that people with common material interests will band together. This is a pragmatic view of ethnicity. An opportunistic allegiance created for a particular common end. Ethnic groups in this view, '....exist essentially as a weapon in pursuit of collective advantage'.[16] Ethnic affinities retain their emotional power so long as they advance shared objective interests.[17]

The primordialist perspective, conversely, portrays ethnicity as deep-seated innate conventions; ethnic communities band together to resist threats of a disorienting environment where rapid change may endanger their culture. While both views are compellingly simple, neither seems able to offer adequate explanations at the level of the individual. Yet it is apparent that the forces which contribute to individual identity and ethnic affinity must be fundamental in an understanding of ethnic relations.

Despres' Multi-dimensional ethnic identity

Despres sees ethnic identity as multi-dimensional phenomena. In an article *'Towards a Theory of Ethnic Phenomena,'* Despres formulated a model (see Appendix 1) which attempts to map out the ambit of an individual's negotiation of ethnic identity within a context of resource competition. It has the advantage of recognising ethnicity and socio-cultural factors as elements of social stratification which construct the individual's identity alongside social class, and institutional structures. Ethnicity is viewed as one form of social stratification, social class is quite another. Ethnic stratifications derive from the status ascribed to different ethnic groups whereas class stratification depends upon achievement in the capitalist economy.[18] Nevertheless, Despres realised that the two organising principles are in reality often united and can coexist.[19] Despres provided avenues for exploration of ethnicity, and admits that the summary model only suggests the value of stratification theory or of a broader theory of power. It is far from clear how such an analysis of levels of differentiation would proceed. Yet the analysis is at heart firmly instrumentalist; tending to see ethnic affinity as an emotional force and a rallying point only in the service of shared objective interests.

Instrumentalist: rational choice

In Guyana the two major ethnic groups have confronted one another in episodes of intense communal violence: and distinct ethnic political constituencies have been formed. Explanations of the motives behind such ethnic collective action include notions of primordial attachment, universalising theories of class and socio-economic structure, and theories of individual psychology focussing on the individual as social actor governed by simple behavioural motives like the avoidance of pain, and the maximisation of pleasure or profit. Theories of rational choice, seek to predict the conditions under which collective action emerges. Such a notion may mark progress over theories of determinism on a grand scale, but rational choice theories seem to assume that humans are primarily involved in maximising gains and avoiding losses.

For example, Hechter, Friedman and Applebaum (1982) perceive collective action as only viable to group members when, '...they estimate that by doing so they will receive a net individual benefit'.[20] Banton's model is claimed to be more realistic, as it focuses on the construction and maintenance of group boundaries. Banton's framework for identifying different group contexts [21] helps to illustrate the matrix of influences which contribute to ethnic identity. Turpin summarises Banton's thesis as the view that '...individuals turn to group support to compensate for reduced privilege as individuals'.[22] The premise that people always act to maximise material and individual advantages may be very much an oversimplification. However, this approach does have the capacity to show broader inter-group and societal dynamics. The unequal access to structures of economic and political power and the constraining influence of the state or dominant ideology is made visible.

Primordialist views

Carter Bentley (1987) summarises the major dichotomy between this pragmatic instrumentalist perspective and primordialist explanations of ethnicity. In the latter, the disruptive effects of rapid change, lead to a sort of collective focus on the essential attributes which uniquely define the group, and provide resistance to a hostile and unstable environment. Pierre Van den Berghe, for example, while he agrees that pluralism can be explained by institutional differences, attributes inter-ethnic conflict to the presence of 'primordial entities' or plural differences.' He has attempted to explain these differences through the agency of socio-biology in such a fashion that, '...seemingly irrational attachments to primordial symbols appear here as the expression of a higher biological rationality.' [23]

Hindu identity

In the case of Guyana, Phillip Singer calls up atavism in his references to the '*Hindu personality*'. The inter-ethnic violence of the Sixties was in his view a 'classic case of communalism.' which meant the 'affirmation of the religious community as a political group'.[24] Claims of this kind are difficult to disprove. However, Bartels argues that, if this inherent cultural force is behind the events in the sixties, why did so many Guyanese, Hindus, who owned prosperous businesses side with Burnham? (the pro African PNC leader) Furthermore, how could large numbers of working class Indians and Africans cooperate successfully during the early days of the PPP? Hindu personality or other primordial attachments do not allow for such examples of cooperation. More recently Kean Gibson re-invoked this type of argument claiming that African-Guyanese rights were being trampled upon by a hierarchically based caste system adhered to by PPP members, through which Africans are perceived as the lowest Shudra caste. Gibson puts forward this primordial explanation for the execution style killings which have been alleged to have been carried out by the Phantom squad

"...the Nazi aim was to beautify the world through violence and thus went from the mass murder of German mental patients and the physically disabled to the mass murder of Jews. The extra-judicial killings in Guyana are not simply a matter of reminding Africans of their place on the social ladder, but to eventually wipe them off the face of the earth so only the civilized will occupy Guyana. Africans are demons and Guyana has to be cleansed of them. The killing of demons is legitimized in the Hindu scriptures. (2003: 60)"

This extreme reliance on primordialist traditions of caste to explain a spate of killings appears to have very little basis in reality; the evidence for secret and conspiratorial caste networks at the highest levels does not seem convincing. While as we will see remnants of caste are recognisable, Gibson's extreme emphasis on secret caste motives seems to be another facet of the deep-seated antipathy felt by African Guyanese towards Indians rather than a scholarly analysis.

Bourdieu's 'Theory of Practice'

Bourdieu's Theory of Practice might allow ethnic relations to be viewed as social and historical codes which, while they shape individual identity and behaviour, are not immutable structures. Rather, they may be seen as part of a repertoire of strategies, which an individual will use, depending on individual as well as larger communal codes of practice to make sense and help negotiation of the social situations s/he is confronted with. The habitus is a product of history and it produces individual and collective practices. It creates the 'active presence of past experiences.' which tend to ensure the 'correctness' of practices and their 'constancy over time.'[25] Bourdieu suggests that the objective conditions of existence - material events in social history - generate the habitus which in turn generate certain dispositions, attitudes and behaviours; a lexicon from which each individual may choose. All such influences are part of the habitus and have been ultimately derived from the history of an individual, a group, or indeed a population. The habitus clearly has features in common with a Marxist notion, that the material conditions giving rise to a social class will be reproduced in the material practices of those experiencing such conditions. At the same time, the habitus can avoid the pitfalls of Marxian and plural society theories which pre-suppose some inevitable cycle of ethnic conflict or class struggle.

Bourdieu's concept of habitus appears to be a valuable theoretical tool. It allows us to take into account both social class and socio-cultural factors. It recognised that all acts of ethnic expression can be explained in terms of lived experiences, habitual practices which produce the codes, and inscribe meanings onto the body and psyche of the individual. It allows us to analyse individuals and groups. There are differences in each individual's habitus. Unique individuals construct their own. However, the individual is also influenced by the specific traditions of a group. The group habitus places limits upon the actions of the individual. It helps to define acceptable behaviour.

'...without violence, art or argument the group habitus tends to exclude all 'extravagances' ('not for the likes of us'), that is, all the behaviours that would be negatively sanctioned because they are incompatible with the objective conditions.'[26]

Because the habitus is a generative structure it is a useful tool to look at cases of inter-ethnic differences, alienation, and conflict which are in a state of constant adjustment and negotiation.

The two major groups in Guyana, in many cases, can be seen to share the same language, speak with enthusiasm about the same aspirations, wear similar clothes, and display many other similarities. Yet although these superficial similarities are often mentioned, they may be rooted in very different generative structures. Bentley comments that...

"Overlaps in the behavioural repertoire of peoples having characteristically different experiences (and habitus) are likely to give rise to invalid assumptions of mutual understanding, what Jurgen Habermas (1970) calls 'systematically distorted communication'." [27]

The culture we live in is far from uniform. There is not a single habitus which affects everything we think, feel and do. Rather, there are a variety of influences upon people. People, notably, behave differently in public and in private spheres. Differences in habitus can lead to conflict and misunderstanding, or selective perception of other group. Conflict and misunderstandings can also occur within groups. If members of the same ethnic community are exposed to different influences, their habitus will be shaped by new experiences, and thus their ability to relate wholeheartedly to the values of their fellows will be affected. The differences may be connected to age group differences, which are commonly noted. For example, if an Indian child attends a local school in which the majority of class-mates are African, then his/her relation to more traditional values will be affected. In a similar way, new popular idioms gain acceptance in the language, a new linguistic repertoire makes it possible to engage in new debates. The word 'sexist,' for example, allowed the opening up of a critical discussion of the treatment of women, which before had little credence. Differences will occur within groups because of such things as education, occupation, regional differences, exposure to different groups, and differences in age. Bourdieu makes the point however, that the agency of change is the habitus itself rather than the category of experience for, '...generation conflicts oppose not age-classes separated by natural properties, but habitus which have been produced by different modes of generation, that is, by conditions of existence which, in imposing different definitions of the impossible, the possible, and the probable, cause one group to experience as natural or reasonable practices or aspirations which another group finds unthinkable or scandalous or vice versa.' [28]

Critique of Bourdieu's Habitus

It has been suggested that the concept of the habitus is too vague and something of a *'black box'*. The *'dispositions'* which Bourdieu says make up the habitus, and which are the 'generative basis' for practices,[29] are not clearly defined. Furthermore, whatever these dispositions are Bourdieu claims they are largely unconscious. This does raise concern, as very often in social situations, people can be seen to be consciously manipulating codes of practice. Furthermore while Bourdieu views the persistence of historical patterns in practice through the mediating role of the habitus, it is, as Jenkins argues,[30] unclear how the largely unconscious *'dispositions'*, acquired through experience, actually produce practices. Nevertheless, Bourdieu has provided a powerful and fertile concept in the habitus. It offers a bridge between social and historical experience on the one hand, and behaviour, values, actions, prejudices and affinities on the other. It further suggests that the manner in which behaviour is expressed (i.e. through the available discourses) and indeed, the elements which are available to be expressed, are constrained by these same social and historical forces. Therefore, Bourdieu's Theory of Practice can cast light upon inter-ethnic relations and the manner in which boundaries are constructed.

Struggle for Symbolic Dominance

In nations like Guyana and Trinidad, ethnic relations may be usefully seen as a struggle for symbolic dominance, the need for a group to establish hegemony through the dissemination and acceptance of the dominant values. In Guyana the series of rapid and disruptive changes in socio-political and economic spheres has contributed to '...the loss of coherence between experience and the symbols through which people understand it'. This in turn, '...causes feelings of discomfort and alienation, of rootlessness and anomie. Both powerful goads to action, hence motives for political mobilisation.'[31]

The leaders of the PNC and the PPP used symbols to establish and reinforce their authority. Their success relied upon them being able to relate to their followers. The 'theory of practice' suggests that '...those leaders will succeed whose personal identity myths resonate with evolving configurations of habitus, practice and experience.'[32] Many writers have suggested that ethnic symbolism is consciously manipulated by an elite. (see Thomas, Premdas, Hintzen and the Latin American Bureau). To obscure the self-serving nature of their activities they erect an ideological screen of shared sentiment with their followers using ethnic symbolism.[33] Given that the electorate are divided along ethnic lines, the leaders of the parties will often use traditional ethnic stereotypes of their opponents.

Political control based on such manipulation of ideology is seen as freezing ethnic relations at a particular point, though it can place limits on the construction of ethnic relations. The defence of political and economic interests shapes habitus. Given that the electorate are divided along ethnic lines, the leaders of the parties will often use traditional ethnic stereotypes of their opponents.

NOTES AND REFERENCES

1   Turpin, T 1990: 73

2   Turpin T. 1990: XVI

3   Smith, R T, 1962, p99.

4   Smith, R T, 1962, p105.

5   Smith, R T, 1962, p198.

6   ibid.

7   Rex, J. 1986, p6

8   Jayawardena, C, 1963, p54.

9   Newman, P, 1964, p79.

10 LaGuerre, J G, 1987, p50.

11 Walks, H, 1979, p2.

12 Smith, M.G. 1982. XIII

13 Turpin, T, 1990, p91.

14 Schermerhorn, 1970, pp58-59.

15 Cohen, R, 1978, p387.

16 Young, C. 1983, p660.

17 Bentley, C. 1987, pp25-26.

18 Despres, L 1975, p195.

19 ibid.

20 Hechter, 1986 in Turpin, 1990, p113.

21 Banton, M. 1983, .

22 Turpin, T. 1990, p114.

23 Bentley, C. 1987, p26.

24 Singer, P, 1967, pp93-116.

25 Bourdieu, P, 1990, p54.

26 Bourdieu, P, 1990:56

27 Bentley, C, 1987: 37

28 Bourdieu, P, 1977, p78.

29 Jenkins, R. 1992, p78.

30 Bourdieu, P, 1992, pp79-97.

31 Bentley, C. 1987, p44.

32 Bentley, C.1987, p41.

33 Brass, 1974, Paterson, 1975, Steinberg, 1981, in Bentley, C, 1987, p41.

CHAPTER 2
Persistence of Ethnic Stereotypes

Racial discourse in Nineteenth Century

The exploitation of *'imported'* peoples in the Caribbean went on for at least 400 years. The barbarism of slavery was replaced by, the only marginally less barbaric, indentureship. The racialisation of differences arguably helped to legitimise the enslavement of people in the harsh regimes of these plantation colonies. The 18th and 19th Centuries saw the creation of pseudo scientific conceptions of race based largely on physical features of different peoples (especially skin colour) and frequently linking such features to ethnocentric perceptions of morality and character.

The culturally constructed order of the natural world appeared to vindicate beliefs about a hierarchy of human types. Linnaeus' taxonomy of the human species, published in 1738, used racial attributes to describe each category. The four human groups which he described were as follows:

- Europeous albus: lively, light, inventive and ruled by rites.
- Americanus Regesceus: tenacious, contented, free, ruled by opinion.
- Asiaticus Luridus: stern, haughty, stingy, ruled by opinion.
- Afer Niger: cunning, slow, negligent, and ruled by caprice.[1]

This type of categorisation was to be found in other popular works of natural history throughout the Eighteenth and Nineteenth centuries (for example see Oliver Goldsmith's Animated Nature, circa.1830, or Baron Cuvier's Animal Kingdom, circa.1890).

Darwin's Origin of Species (1859), while it led to a recognition of the non-uniqueness of the human race, also gave the rationale for a racially stratified view of evolution - based on an ethnocentric colonial view of the subjugated nations by their relative lack of Western technology were deemed more lowly. Europeans represented the highest point of evolution, diverse Asians and Indians fell in somewhere behind, and Africans brought up the rear.[2]

Racial Categorisation in Guyana

The colonists arriving in Guyana, firstly the Dutch and then the British, brought with them prescribed hierarchical values which they believed put them legitimately at the top of a ladder of creation. Prior to the British seizure of the colony in 1802, the Dutch had been colonial masters for nearly two hundred years. Along with the French and Spanish they had been active in importing slaves from Africa, having found the Amerindians too hard to enslave.

The Africans having been forcibly divested of their living traditions - languages, religious beliefs and kinship systems, came to form *'Creole'* communities intermarrying with Amerindians. The treatment of both the indigenous peoples and the Africans imported as slaves was frequently marked by ruthless and inhuman treatment. There were uprisings against these conditions; notably the Berbice rebellion of 1763 which was defeated, not by the Dutch, but by a dispute between leaders of the rebel slaves. Although slavery was finally abolished in 1834, the freed slaves were forced to serve a period of *'apprenticeship'* for a further six years. This led to further protests and demonstrations. The scheme was abandoned in 1838, and the Africans were expelled from the plantations. Although it was expulsion, there is a popular misconception that Guyanese left willingly, and were reluctant to work on the site of their previous enslavement. However, Jagan indicates that the exodus from plantations was in many cases due to the planters' refusal to provide security of tenure to provision farmers on their lands. (Typically vegetables like eddo, cassava, callalloo, etc.)[3] The level of cooperative enterprise which the African-Guyanese attained under these trying circumstances was an impressive achievement.

By 1851, the Africans throughout the colony had erected 11,152 houses, and the property owned by them was worth nearly £1 million pounds. Of the 60,000 Africans and mulattoes then in the colony, about two thirds had migrated to the villages.[4] These changes created a severe labour shortage for the planters and other groups were sought to fill the vacuum. Portuguese were initially brought in, 469 by 1835. However, the importation of white Europeans to work alongside Africans created contradictions in the perceived social order. Therefore, other groups were sought and in 1838, 396 Indians arrived. These Indian labourers, who came to form the largest migrant group after the emancipation, were looked upon by the Africans as alien interlopers. On one hand the influx of the cheap labour the Indians provided undercut the Africans' struggle for wage labour and took away the opportunity for them to obtain part-time work on the plantations. On the other hand, the Portuguese soon established themselves as a mercantile class and were able to import cheap foodstuffs, which undermined the Africans' attempts to establish themselves as provision farmers.

'Between 1838 and 1850 former slaves, who had won their freedom in 1838, purchased numerous abandoned sugar plantations and constituted themselves into *'a peasant class'*. This group shared antagonistic class relations with the planter oligarchy because they competed for labour, capital (state assistance and private funding), arable lands, access to technology and subsequently, for political power'.[5]

Colonial Segregation – 'Divide and Rule'

Not only was the culture of the Indian labourer alien and incomprehensible to the existing Guyanese (most of the Indians to enter Guyana were and still are Hindus) but they posed an economic threat to African-Guyanese struggling to compete for wage labour. The newly contracted Indian workers were in most cases placed in villages, created to serve the various plantations. This planted the seeds of physical segregation. These villages were almost exclusively Indian. 'There were of course villages where Indians and Africans lived together (or at least side by side) but on the whole the two groups formed separate enclaves'.[6]

It has frequently been argued that colonial regimes depend on this type of segregationist policy to maintain their authority. For example Gonzalez maintains that, '...racism and racial segregation are essential in the colonial exploitation of some peoples by others. They influence all configurations of development in colonial cultures...'[7] The claim here is that in Guyana a range of factors existed, which created the conditions for the development of distinct African and Indian identities. These include, firstly, segregation by the planters; separating physically the African (Creole) from the Indian. Secondly, the whole context into which the Indians arrived was one of competitiveness and antagonism. This bitter climate was created by an aggressive colonial power which reinforced itself by engendering divisions between the imported groups. One source of virulent stereotypical images, at this point, was the planters themselves. Their often derogatory and racist discourse served to demean and undermine time-honoured traditions of both Africans and Indians.

Colonialism: African and Indian Stereotypes

Walter Rodney notes that planter propaganda in the Nineteenth century, which focused on the Indian labourers was in fact, '...a repetition of the caricature of the African under slavery.'[8] The African stereotype figure was called *'Quashie'* (a corruption of the name Kwesi, a West African ruler) who was characterised as indomitably lazy, yet endowed with huge virility and strength, '... cutting tons of cane and producing when the work horses failed in the Demerara mud.'[9] Another account referred to by Banton states that the '... typical Negro was poor Quashee, a swift, supple fellow; a merry-hearted, grinning, dancing, singing, affectionate kind of creature, with a great deal of melody and amenability in his composition'.[10] The Africans, however, had largely embraced English values marking their ascent out of slavery. Many migrated to the towns and became wage earners, taking up lowly posts in the civil service and the police force. Smith points out that the '... African-Guyanese population congregated into church based communities, becoming imbued with the values of respectability and 'English culture' which they used to differentiate themselves from the Indian indentured sugar workers.'[11]

It seems the plantocracy constructed an equally contradictory image of the Indian. The Indian holy man, the Swamy, was belittled in the popular stereotype of the Indian *'Sammy'*, and attributed the same contradictory traits as *'Quashie'*; at once violent yet childlike in dependency, hard working yet thievish, admirably frugal yet miserly to the point of self neglect. Despite the apparent differences between the two groups, and the understandable animosity, they shared many of the same lived experiences.

Creolisation

Rodney describes the process of 'Creolisation' as a, '...counter force to incommensurable cultural differences, particularly in its effects upon the younger generation of Indians'. While the term *'creole'* (used everyday in Guyana) refers to people of African or part African descent, *'creolisation'* refers to the transforming influence exerted by Creole culture on any other ethnic group. Rodney gives several examples of aspects of daily life which have assisted in the development of shared habitus.

One of the more evocative uses of the word 'Creole' in a Guyanese context, is its association with the '...Creole gang that comprised children who did manuring and other light field tasks as soon as they were physically able so to do. It was the earliest socialising work experience and was one of the imperatives of indigenisation.'[12]

Indians in Guyana have been concerned with maintaining Indian culture and resisting wholesale creolisation. The recognition of cultural differences creates stereotypes about the nature and actions of the 'coolie' and the 'blackman'. '...Ethnic conflict occurs in terms of criticisms, ridicule and invidious comparison of these stereotypes.'[13] Interestingly while some Indians maintain what they would view as traditional culture, the process of creolisation has inevitably brought about gradual change (and of course cultural shifts have occurred in language, cuisine, religious practices etc) which over a century and a half have made Indians into Indian-Guyanese, who would be quite different to Indian Hindus or Moslems in India. This is the nature of diasporas; there is often a yearning for an imagined homeland, and a distorted or idealised memory which can never be re-gained.

Although there were mutually exclusive elements within African and Indian groups in Guyana, their cultures have influenced one another. The plantation experience inscribed similar conditions on both the indentured Indian and the Creole Africans. It is significant that upon leaving the estates, Indians are said to have behaved just as emancipated Africans had previously. These aspects of cultural convergence were embodied in the responses to the material existence and the work environment of both groups. 'Taken in its broadest sense, the *'culture'* of the racial fractions of the working people included their work environment, and their responses to capital at the point of production. In these critical areas, Africans and free Indians were on common ground'.[14]

British colonial values

The facts of shared degradation at the hands of colonial overseers, and the British colonial values which permeated the educational, religious, and commercial institutions in the colony have left their mark on the Guyanese character (Indian or African). David De Caries (Editor of the Stabroek News) underlined the extent of the impact of British values on the Guyanese personality, when he commented, '..If we look at the essence of the Guyanese personality what do we find huh? A middle class Englishman? Not quite, but there have been those influences; the parliamentary system, the notion of fair play, the legal system, and so on.'[15]

The fact that the Indians were the latecomers to the colony meant in effect that they were taking the bottom place which the Africans had filled in the colonists' eyes. It also meant that they were slower in emerging to embrace the dominant European values, to have access into the education system, and hence the lower rungs of the social ladder. This ascent towards white European respectability (which involves taking on a contradictory set of values) was already happening for many African-Guyanese, as they moved into the urban areas.

Premdas has made a study of the manner in which voluntary organisations like The League of Coloured Peoples, The East Indian Association, the European Club, and many others have served to maintain cultural boundaries between different groups.[16] Moreover, these sorts of associations, catering to specific cultural needs of the respective communities, were reflected in the role of the different churches.

Historical Basis for Stereotypes of Indian-Guyanese

Indians arriving in the colony under the indentureship scheme had accepted a contract which bound them to the rigors of plantation work for a fixed period, and under conditions which were not far removed from those which slaves had laboured. Despite the appalling conditions of transportation and labour in which many died, it could be argued that the voluntary nature of indentureship was less destructive of cultural values than slavery, and much of the original culture remained intact. It seems that this separation may have been partly engineered by the colonial authorities. Braithwaite argues that many of the cultural traditions or at least the visible aspects of Indian culture- language, food, dress, religious rites and festivals and so on- were retained almost intact from the ancestral home.[17]

Moore's study of racial attitudes in Nineteenth Century plantation society reveals the enmity which existed between the two groups. He claimed that there was '... no denying the fact that there exists an uncalled for bitter feeling between the native Creole and the Indian immigrant towards each other'.[18] The exchange of roles, in which Indian migrants worked in the fields and were billeted in some of the same rude quarters the freed blacks remembered with such aversion, deem to have aroused various emotions in Africans. On the one hand the Indians were perceived as '...semi-savages or semi-civilised barbarians from a barbarous country, they were simply 'coolies' or 'matiyon', porters, day labourers, burden carriers'.[19] On the other hand they were not popular, as their presence undermined the African's struggle for wage labour, and took away for many the option of supplementing income by part-time work on the plantations. Furthermore, the colonists took advantage of, and helped to maintain, the existing tensions between the two groups, by having each group police the other. The Africans, however, had largely embraced English values marking their ascent out of slavery. Many migrated to the towns and became wage earners, taking up lowly posts in the civil service and the police force.

The Indians were also distanced from the European and Creole community, by the fact that the elementary education system was ineffective and made little impression upon those confined to the lowest rungs of society. The newly arrived Indians would have been reluctant to send their children to schools in which polluting European values might have been propagated. Indeed as R. T .Smith (1982) and others have noted, the Indians in Guyana and Trinidad remained largely uneducated until after World War II. Their isolation was further compounded by an active policy of residential segregation. The planters even had Hindu and Moslem temples built to accommodate the religions of their workers.[20] This sort of divide and rule was a common experience for both groups, '...each group at different times came to understand what it meant to be at the total mercy of planters in the plantation logies of the nigger-yard and the bound yard.' [21]

Despite common experience, stereotypes of difference developed and fed into mutual contempt. The Creoles would not even contribute to charitable collections made for the Indians by Creole churches because Indians were held to be beneath even charity. One contemporary anecdote related that on hearing of the tragic drowning of six Indians, a Christian Creole woman simply dismissed it as '...Coolies! Only coolies! Tchups! I thought you were speaking of people!' [22]

Braithwaite believes that the Indian was protected from reacting with self contempt through the maintenance of a very distinct culture. The Indians preserved their taboos and rules about food, and '... religion gave him values which were not the white values of the rest of the community, and preserved him from self-contempt.'[23] Furthermore, the disciplinary ordering of plantation society imposed a very repressive regime which also separated the Indian from other groups. Freedom of movement was severely restricted. Their homes could be invaded at any time and they could be forced out to work. Their place was either at work, in hospital or in jail.[24]

Stereotypes developed which cast the Indian men as potentially violent towards their wives. Brereton, in her work, noted the evolution of stereotypes about Indian migrants. '...Insulation and separateness fed exaggerated notions of real cultural differences. For example, a moral panic arose over the so called 'coolie wife murders', murders which occurred because, 'Indian men believed they had the right to kill unfaithful wives. A notion quite alien to the Africans - who had infinitely more casual ideas about sex and marriage.'[25] This notion of Indian violence arising from the *'wife murders'* has persisted and is prevalent in popular perceptions of Indians in Guyana. Traditionally strict rules of exogamy and ignorance of Hindu ceremonies, involving sacrifices may have fuelled its persistence. Smith observed that, the African's stereotype of the Indian is that these people would do anything for money, and that this money is hoarded rather than used to improve their life style.

The single-mindedness of the Indians to save money and forego present comforts and the good life for future improvement and security, is often condemned as avarice and causes irritation to the Europeans and the Africans alike.[26]

The Historical Basis for Stereotypes of African-Guyanese

The Indians view of African-Guyanese is equally distrustful. Indeed the popular Indian stereotype of the African forms almost a complementary opposite to the African view of Indians. To understand the manner in which popular Indian stereotypes of Africans emerged, it is necessary to consider more than simply the struggle with African rivals for waged labour. The Indian attitudes towards African-Guyanese might be influenced by other factors. Several Guyanese writers have suggested that the Indian would have formed the same negative opinion of the African-Guyanese, even if the colonial and socio-economic conditions had not been so divisive.

Caste

Haraksingh has claimed that the legacy of the caste system has a direct bearing on ethnic relations in Guyana even today. He believes that a notional form of caste hierarchy still exerts influence on Indian perceptions of Africans, a system which has been elaborated and instilled in Indians over the centuries, and, moreover, '... a system which far from being static and inflexible has always been able to incorporate and give a place to new elements.' [27] has been instrumental in providing Indians with an inbuilt scale, a way of ascribing to groups a specific place in a hierarchy.

'This place is determined by the ritual status of the group, which in turn, depends on the concept of ritual purity and pollution. The more ritually impure a group is judged to be, the lower the position which it is accorded in the hierarchy'.[28] Haraksingh outlines the essential criteria for judging ritual purity as: birth, occupation, customs, and habits. A caste member shares a place in the caste hierarchy with the group into which he is born. Each group has a myth of origin and is associated with a specific type of occupation, and certain customs and habits. In Trinidad the indentured Indians evaluating the Africans by each of these standards found them irredeemably polluted. Their culinary habits, eating of pork and beef (taboo to Muslims and Hindus respectively) and their employment - many Africans worked in the leather industry (a defiled substance) were examples of their lowliness and defilement.

The adaptability of the caste system is illustrated by the ready manner in which Indians incorporated the existence of Africans into their canon of beliefs, and devised a myth to explain their origins. 'They were supposed to have been adherents of Ravana in his inglorious struggle against Rama. The monkey god Hanuman, faithful servant of Ravana, tied a burning cloth to his tail and swished it through the air. The flames darkened the negroes skins of Ravana's followers and curled their hair. Negroes were therefore identified with the ungodly and the polluted. (Haraksingh, 1974:68)

According to this view the Africans in Trinidad and Guyana would have been considered as an additional Indian caste, as another class of untouchables. While Haraksingh agrees that caste has lost much of its significance, he believes that vestiges of the system have survived the experience of indentureship in an alien society. The existing notional caste system, he believes, is still influential in maintaining boundaries, especially in such areas as inter-marriage. He accepts that there may be some merit in Brereton's argument about the evolution of stereotypes, but believes that the Indian perception of Africans as the pariah caste has more explanatory adequacy, '...than if they were seen simply as being determined by stereotypical notions formed during the early days of contact.'[29]

It certainly seems reasonable to accept that some form of caste system has prevailed and may have contributed actively to the segmentation of Guyanese society. Yet it must be remembered that although the transplanted cultural values partly blocked and filtered out the effects of 'creolisation', even by the end of the nineteenth century, Creole influence had permeated many areas of Indian life. The Indian in his loin cloth, the object of derision to the Creole population who had grasped the next rung of the social ladder and increasingly adopted the English values of the planters, was no longer seen. Aspects of diet, speech and even funeral customs were all modified to the new cultural codes in which the Indians came to make their lives.

Caste in the accepted sense of a 'defined system of structured relationships' was clearly untenable in Guyana. Rauf argues however that there is a deep structure to caste which could be said to have endured. He claims:

'The social, political, economic and juridical relations among the members of the East Indian community are not based on caste lines. The early demographic imbalance and working conditions on plantations made the survival of the caste based structure of Indian society impossible.' [30]

However, Rauf argues (and Haraksingh lends support to this) that while the Indian community as a whole became more or less a single caste, members of other ethnic groups, the Portuguese, Chinese, Africans, and Amerindians, were in fact perceived as separate castes with whom quite distinct social relationships were established.

Eusi Kwayana, a foundation member of the People's Progressive Party and presently a leading figure in the Working People's Alliance, made the following comments when asked about the survival of a *'notional'* caste identity.

'Some Indians are very slow to accept that ideas of caste persist; I myself believe that they do. In my time I have known things like colour to operate within the Hindu-Guyanese community. I knew when fair Indians and dark Indians began to marry; I noted that. And when relations go sour they will still talk of this caste and that caste and the so called non-high caste or low caste people very often refer to the Brahmins critically - they play a negative political role from the point of view of the lower caste. They say 'Uh that's how these people behave, typical of a Brahmin'. And it works both ways. I won't say that it determines anything major in Indian communities these days, but it is there lurking in the background. If they have caste within themselves, in what appears to other people to be simply Indian - you can understand the difficulty of integrating with those who are entirely non-Indian - that is an even greater leap and has to be a much greater experience.' [31]

This persistence, and adaptation of structures of caste into a new set of contingencies illustrates again the manner in which habitus operates. It ensures the active presence of past experiences, which deposited in each organism in the form of schemes of perception, thought and action, tend to guarantee the 'correctness of practices and their constancy over time, more reliably than all formal rules and explicit norms.' [32] It is clear from the example of caste that this process is very far from being a mere mechanical reproduction of past structures. Furthermore, the gradual diminution of power of caste indicates that although such inscribed dispositions are tenacious, changes which unfold in the conditions of the everyday lives of people are likely to generate changes in the habitus itself. While the claims about caste based identity are unrealistic, entrenched stereotypical views of Indian-Guyanese clearly persist.

Evidence that such feelings are still prevalent was evinced from my own recordings of attitudes in Guyana, in 1991. There were numerous occasions when Africans portrayed Indians as niggardly, even to the point of self-deprivation, so single-minded was their hunger for wealth. In two months of field notes I recorded over 30 negative references from Africans in regard to the perceived greed and scheming nature of Indian-Guyanese. Behind mere frequency there is a depth of negative feeling associated with the stereotype, as revealed in the following exchange, typical of those from my notes.

During a conversation with two African-Guyanese professionals, Larry and Geoff, in the emotionally charged atmosphere of the Demico House bar in central Georgetown, the following exchange took place after a discussion of a high profile Indian business man, Yesu Persaud. Neither of my companions rated this figure highly. Geoff said, 'You see in the land of the blind the one-eyed man king'.

Larry called him a *'lackney'*. Then they took turns in attacking his credibility. He was given his house by President Burnham as part of an immoral deal. Without any prompting the invective started to flow, both men seemed suddenly excited, needled by my off-hand question about this much-lauded Indian entrepreneur. There was much thumping of the table. Geoff reached for my empty bottle and said:

'Say the Indian wants your bottle - or wot not. He will be so nice - so very good to you, you would never know. He will offer you money, and if that doesn't work - he will send his daughter to you, and if you don't want her he will send his wife! And as soon as he achieve this end - he take it away, then you know he never speak to you again - never! He only interested in the money. That's how they are.'

I ventured that this was perhaps a generalisation and that surely some Indians had other motives. Larry could barely contain his impatience; *'It is general mon! They all the same - ALL!'* (Recorded in Georgetown, 5/3/1991)

Such vehement expressions of resentment are commonplace and reflect the Indians apparent ease, relative to many Africans, at managing financial matters and property, causing jealousy and condemnation.

The single-mindedness of the Indians to save money and forego present comforts and the good life for future improvement and security, was condemned as avarice and caused irritation to the whites and the Africans alike. (Vasil, 1984: 243)

The persistence of African-Guyanese stereotypes

The fears of many Indians seemed to focus on the common perception of the African as overly physical and their dominance also perhaps *'physically'* manifest in the state itself (especially through the use of coercive force to maintain their power base). This stereotype was notably strong around Georgetown, the seat of government, where African-Guyanese are in the majority. There was a wide-spread feeling amongst the Indians that they were vulnerable to attack by Africans. The blame for all muggings, known as *'choke and rob'* and break-ins known as *'kick down door'* was always assigned to *'Blackmen'* by Indians.

The following is an extract from an encounter with a Georgetown East Indian man in his early twenties who worked as a mini-bus *'conductor'*. The exchange took place on an empty bus, the only other person present was the Indian driver.

SS "Do you feel that there is any racist attitude? ..."

Indian man (Ind) "Racist. Yes! Racialism - there is! Yeah very strong. You see the Negro people - them don't - them ain't got this kina way - like you know, building a future. Them only brek it - them ain't got dis ting so. They people avent got the stronghold over this country - is East Indian people and Portuguese - people like Peter D'Aguair..."

SS "Right I see ..."

Ind. "... like Kayman Sankur and Yesu Persuad. Majority is Indian or Portuguese - but no you don't find no black people getting capital investment in this country. Any investment they got - they responsible for is drug pusher..."

SS "Drug pusher - Yeah?"

Ind. "Yeah they jus getting the money - look you'd ah seen em on the streets, riding the most fanciest bike, the most fanciest car to drive in. They dress their self in gold right?"

SS "Uh huh. Yes"

Ind. "They dress their self in gold - Indian can't wear gold and the Negro would wear them in town on the skin. Why? They bully - cause if you wear it they come an choke you. They don't do this no more (Here he demonstrated a choke and rob hold on my neck) Years ago they used to choke you..."

SS "Choke and rob - yeah?"

Ind. "... and rob you. Now. Now. They cutting you off! They cutting your finger off and they walking alongside you on the pave and they just take out the knife of the pocket ... 'and dis don't move' – one on one side - now you can feel something sharp sticking in your side - 'now don't move' - a sudden movement (he became increasingly agitated here-) Very bully - black people very very very bully! Black people travelling in this veekle - they arlways shart of money and they need music - they need spacious seat - and they arlways short of   money. Yes." (Georgetown 13 April 1991).

This sense of vulnerability appears to have – if anything increased. Since the PPP achieved government in 1992 there have been allegations there a great many aggravated assaults and murders in Guyana are racially motivated and largely perpetrated by African-Guyanese against Indians. (see discussion of crime in next chapter).

Apart from the overt sense of physical threat here, which illustrates the common stereotype of the African as a physical aggressor, there is also reference to another popularly voiced view of the African as profligate, flashy and lacking in sound financial judgement.

"For Indians, the *'economic irresponsibility'* stereotype is not peculiar to a segment of the African population, but is true of all Africans generally".[24]

The Indians frequently portray any African as in some way culturally inferior. One respondent gestured angrily at the defaced statue of Victoria and said, 'See what they done to the mother.' There is a story, almost a social and political allegory, which I heard from several Indians, that when the African-Guyanese leader Burnham finally got into office one of his first acts was the almost ritual desecration of this colonial icon. He had it tossed into the ditch at the back of the parliament buildings and, or so a number of Indian respondents claimed, defecated on the statue.

Indian professionals also seemed unable to resist the occasional belittling joke or comment about the African, usually with reference to the violent or animal nature of the African as stylised elements in the jokes.

Whether such attitudes are the partial legacy of caste beliefs which portray Africans as unclean or they stem from economic and political struggles, or indeed a complex interaction of many factors, they are certainly prevalent. In my field notes over a period of two months, I recorded over twenty references to these alleged qualities which were attributed to African-Guyanese by Indians.

Apart from the overt sense of physical threat here, which illustrates the common stereotype of the African as a physical aggressor, there is also reference to another popularly voiced view that of the African as profligate, flashy and lacking in sound financial judgement.

The other's theft of legitimate pleasures

Slavoj Zizek (1990) uses the phrase *'Theft of Enjoyment'* to explain the complex psycho-social perception of the other. In the article he related this notion to the growing tensions in the former Yugoslavia. Zizek equates national movements and 'causes' with the manner in which ethnic groups, *'...organise their enjoyment through national myths'*.[36] Further he presents the notion of the other constantly impinging on our senses because of their perceived lack of restraint in the practice of their pleasures. In the racist perspective, the *'other'* is either a workaholic stealing our jobs or an idler living on our labour, and it is quite amusing to note the ease with which one passes from reproaching the *'other'* with a refusal to work to reproaching him for the theft of work.

The two views of the other as related by Zizek above can equally be seen in the African and Indian-Guyanese stereotypes of each other. Indian-Guyanese often fear the African population believing that they are responsible for robbery and street crimes which are especially grievous when related to the loss of their pleasure in adorning themselves with gold and jewellery in public, which was once an important aspect of the culture. Conversely, African-Guyanese feel the Indians success and facility with money and property is a direct trespass on the pleasure and privilege to which their traditional status as public service workers entitled them. Indians are seen as workaholics. Their ambitions are often viewed as avaricious, and their willingness to save money single-mindedly, and to sacrifice the comforts of the good life of the present as meanness.[37]

There is the constant nagging discomfort for the African-Guyanese that Indians are stealthily taking what is the African birthright as the longest serving group in Guyana, through fair means or foul. The African-Guyanese feel a unique right in their political ascendancy. Their guarantee of jobs in the civil service is perceived as being under threat from the success of Indian-Guyanese who have gained more of a foot-hold in the public service as well as in the professions and in business. The Indians by contrast have been denied access to the higher levels of government as the public service; the *'corridors of power'* have been the protected domain of PNC members.

Brim Pollard an African-Guyanese executive of CARICOM [38] felt that the Indian population was now undermining what the Africans had long viewed as their just rewards as the true *'natives'* of Guyana. He admitted that he felt anxious himself, although he recognised it was irrational. He spoke of the Indians as *'up and coming'* in commerce and the public service, astute and hungry for power.[39]

The maintenance of boundaries through the use of stereotyped images is not a peripheral activity governed by caprice, but rather an activity central to one's own identity and security in a recognisable social world. Classifying the other by reference to their body, size, shape, diet, economic behaviours and so on, is essential in defining one's own social space. '...Nothing classifies somebody more than the way he or she classifies.' [40] Such images are the boundary markers of identity for the individual member of an ethnic group. They are ways of envisaging the other and hence oneself.

NOTES AND REFERENCES

1   Young, C. 1976, p50.

2   Young, C. 1976, p50.

3   Jagan, C. 1997, p34.

4   ibid

5   Rose, J. 1989, p51.

6   Braithwaite, L, 1974, p44.

7   Casonova, G in Manley R,, 1979, p85.

8   Rodney, W, 1981, p180.

9   ibid

10   Banton, M 1967, p25.

11   Ross, 1982, p112.

12   Rodney, W, 1981, p178.

13   Jayawardena, C, 1963, p54.

14   Rodney, W, 1981, p179.

15   Interview, 3.4.1991

16   Premdas, R, 1981, 44

17   L, Braithwaite, 1974,

18   Bronkhurst in, B, Moore, 1987, p179.

19   ibid.

20   Singh, C, 1988, p9.

21   Rodney, W, 1981, p178.

22   Bronkhurst in Moore, B, 1987, p179.

23   An East Indian's view quoted in Braithwaite, L, 1974

24   Jagan, C, 1997, p40.

25   Bereton, B, 1974, p20.

26   Vasil, Raj K, 1984, p243.

27   Interview with Kusha Haraksingh, 18 March 1991.

28   Haraksingh, K, 1974, p68.

29   ibid.

30   Rauf, M 1974, p95.

31   Interview with Eusi Kwayana, WPA HQ, Georgetown, 21 April 1991.

32   Bourdieu, P, 1977, p54.

33   Singer, P, 1967, pp93-116.

34   Premdas, R, 1972: 290-291

35   Premdas, R,1972b, pp290-291.

36   Zizeck, S, 1990, p4.

37   Vasil, R K, 1984, p243.

38   The Caribbean equivalent to the EEC.

39   Interview in Georgetown 2 April 1994.

40   Bourdieu, P, 1988, p132

CHAPTER 3
Political parameters of ethnicity in Guyana

In Guyana communal rivalry accelerated and ethnic boundaries became more emphatic and strongly visible, in the race to gain political power prior to independence. Expressions of ethnic identity in Guyana's turbulent post-colonial era have often focused upon or been drawn into the struggle for nationhood. The excessive investment of the political machinery in distinct ethnic constituencies served to reinforce traditional stereotypes.

Stereotypes play an important role in identity formation, providing negative ethnic attributes which serve as boundary markers between Africans and Indians. Ethnic identity then appears to be frequently defined through such mythical constructions of the *'other'*, and the struggle for political dominance has surrounded such attributes with increased bitterness and vehemence. But the primary point here is that these boundaries, which seem so formative in individual and group identity, are not merely evoked to gain political or economic advantage, they are deep-seated dispositions created by historically evolving habitus. Certain elements (shared history, life experiences under colonial rule) make up a super-ordinate Guyanese habitus; but other elements (cultural origins, divisive colonial practices, religious beliefs, and the struggle to eke out an existence under very difficult and competitive circumstances) have produced quite distinct generative structures. It appears that political forces can evoke either set of elements within the Guyanese psyche.

Political divisions

On the 7th of October 1992 The People's Progressive Party (PPP) finally achieved power after twenty eight years of rule by the People's National Congress (PNC), a regime marked by consistent vote rigging and other non-democratic and coercive practices. Each of these parties came to represent an ethnic bloc. The PPP became the Indian party, and the PNC was the pro-African faction that split away in 1955. The period since the early 1960's, with the attendant violence and ethnic struggle between the African and Indian-Guyanese, has inevitably been construed as proof of the pluralist thesis. Pluralists were confidently asserting[1] that Marxist theory was irrelevant as ethnicity was the primary site of cleavage. Indeed the pluralist theory gained such prestige that it even led to calls for partitioning the country along ethnic lines, and creating a sort of mutual apartheid. Pluralists, such as Furnival and later M.G. Smith, shared a common view that ethnic groups will inevitably display antagonism and rivalry when integration has not occurred.

Certainly ethnic relations in Guyana have been marked by competition for scarce resources, but the picture of unfolding events in Guyana could not be seen solely as a case of ethnic mobilisation to maximise gains for the ethnic groups. In fact neither pluralist nor Marxist simplifications seem adequate as accounts of Guyana's recent history.

Stages in the development of ethnic relations in Guyana

Guyana's political history may be narrated in three distinct stages, with defined core characteristics, as Premdas (1986) has suggested: First Guyana developed as a multi-ethnic society under the control of a colonial power, in which the dominant values were those of the European elite. Second, after almost a century this monopoly was broken as the non-European ethnic groups pushed for reforms, and gradual liberalisation of the franchise was achieved. As the colonial order was challenged and finally expelled, 'full scale competition for the preferred values of government activity ensued. Intense conflict between the ethnic segments developed for power, jobs, projects and security; this conflict was translated at the national level as competitive party politics'.[2] Third, the pro-African PNC engineered a victory, with the connivance of outside interests (US and British governments) and held full sway over the instruments of state. The PNC attempted to impose its ideological values and controls on the society, though ultimately failing in the latter.[3] This history suggests that ethnic constituencies remain intact despite some attempts to re-focus attention away from racial identification, and the likely movement will be a vacillation between ethnic enclaves The PPP regained power after the 1992 and again in 97 and 2002; the later elections being occasions for violence and allegations of rigged voting.

1953 - 1962

The violent disturbances of the late 1950's and early 1960's altered the intensity of political and ultimately of ethnic divisions in Guyana at both grass root and executive levels. Two figures have dominated the politics of Guyana from the 1940s to the present day; Dr Cheddi Jagan and Forbes Burnham. Burnham, a London-trained lawyer, gained a reputation for Machiavellian politics and impressive powers of oration. He was active in the trade union movement and became a founding member of the People's Progressive Party, contributing to the movements' growing influence, by adding the support of African workers to the predominantly Indian membership. An article entitled, 'Beware My Brother Forbes' (written by his sister Jessie, and suppressed by the authorities) describes Forbes as having *a certain slickness, a sly glibness'*. The short pamphlet published before the elections in 1964, which began his twenty one year reign as Comrade Leader of Guyana, is an exhortation to think twice before casting a vote for Burnham. The PPP, the first mass political party, was formed in 1950 under the leadership of Dr Jagan with Forbes Burnham as chairman.

Jagan the son of a driver on the Port Mourant sugar estate in Berbice, strongly identified with the sugar workers. Returning from the US in 1943 (as a doctor of dentistry) he became a militant among the sugar estates, especially those on the East Coast of Demerara. Unlike other Indian leaders who were generally urban based, Jagan won a seat in the Legislative Council through his staunch campaigning for improved conditions for sugar workers.

In 1953 the first general elections were held under universal adult suffrage, and there was a great deal of popular interest in the campaigning. Opposition to the PPP came from a variety of independents and splinter groups, and the more established NDP (National Democratic Party) which represented the establishment including churches and big business. In *The West on Trial*, Jagan relates one of the first incidents of race used in political campaigning:

'The NDP and the League of Coloured People attempted to woo support away from us by appealing to African racism. Their propaganda line was simple enough - the PPP was Indian dominated, and Burnham, an African, was only being used. On the other hand, in the countryside, the Indian voters were told that I was sacrificing the interests of Indians and selling out to the Africans.' [4]

However, the PPP won a decisive victory in 1953 (winning 18 out of 24 seats). Divisions became apparent after the victory when Burnham held up the business of selecting ministers by demanding the leader be chosen first. Jagan saw this as a transparent scheme on Burnham's part to be *'leader or nothing'*. However, his bid for leadership was thwarted as the General Council returned Jagan as leader, with Burnham retaining his role as chairman. The newly elected government retained office for only 133 days.

During this period the PPP brought about much needed reforms in an attempt to redress the appalling social conditions suffered by many agricultural workers; and there was legislation to further secure fair labour relations and political independence. Furthermore, the PPP made no secret of their intentions to nationalise key foreign companies and dismantle the entrenched colour-class system. The proposed reforms were said to prove communist infiltration.

The colonial Governor used his right of veto and suspended the constitution ostensibly because the PPP was setting up a one party communist state. However, it seems clear now that this was a pretext for the fear of losing the lucrative revenue from sugar and minerals (see Curtis, M. 2003) Police and British troops were given extensive powers to enter people's homes to search for *'communists'*. As a result two opposing factions formed in the ranks of the PPP; one following Burnham, the other Jagan. After the propaganda[5] and moral panic which attended the suspension of the constitution, PPP leaders were victimised; both Jagan and his wife Janet were given 6 month sentences for violating restriction orders.

Burnham, although he ignored restriction orders, was never arrested. The internal rift within the PPP led to an irrevocable division in 1955 when the Burnhamite faction formed into a separate party, the People's National Congress (PNC).

Despite the fact that Jagan's PPP managed to win general elections up until 1961, the communist scare served to divide the national movement, distance the middle class, and mobilise the conservative elements and church groups. Undoubtedly Jagan himself did little to allay fears as he persisted with his strongly Marxist pronouncements. This also allowed ample rhetorical space for Burnham to formulate a moderate *'social democrat'* platform.

By early 1964 it was clear that *'communalism'* much more than *'communism'* was the obstacle to independence and that '... Dr Jagan's party had by now changed, in fact if not in rhetoric, from an anti-colonial radical front into an Indian organisation.' [6]   Similarly, the PNC now reflected a defensive African-Guyanese opinion, much more than Burnham's modified socialism. Superficially, this seems to indicate a trend towards increasing polarisation, but it can be argued that deep-seated differences have always existed between the Indians and Africans in Guyana and were only now finding political expression.

In an interview, Dr Bassier, an anthropologist at the University of Guyana, supported this view, feeling strongly that the early PPP was never really a united front, and the source of the divisions in the PPP was not the suspension of the constitution but lay much deeper. Dr Bassier (who has made a close study of ethnic divisions in Guyana) claimed that Jagan was supported by the Indian population and Burnham by the African population. These separate constituencies helped to secure the success of the PPP. It is fallacious, he argues, to assume that there was anything other than superficial cooperation between African and Indian-Guyanese people before the strife of the 1960's.[7]

However, the Commonwealth Commission investigating the violence in 1962 '...found little evidence of any racial segregation in the social life of the country...' Indeed they went on to claim that 'East Indians and Africans seemed to mix and associate with one another on terms of the greatest cordiality...' The suggestion was that the *'racial twist'* had been played upon by unscrupulous politicians.[8]

1962 – 1964

From 1962 up until the elections in 1964, Guyana was wracked by inter-ethnic violence. Out of a population of 700,000, it is estimated that over 700 were killed in this period. Perry Mars, a leading Guyanese academic made a study of this period, and suggests that it was more extensively violent than any other in the modern era of Guyana's history. A primary reason for this, Mars suggests, is that ethnic polarisation was pronounced:

'Racial tensions were politically exploited mainly through ethnic based organisations, which led to a kind of mutual elimination contest between African and Indian-Guyanese. The result was an almost total polarisation, which even meant migration into ethnically distinct geographical areas. The real tragedy of this process was the disintegration of an increasing trend toward the development of multi-ethnic communities up to that time.' [9]

Dennis Bassier also gave evidence of this cross-migration between different villages:

'In their quest for political supremacy I think the PNC did a lot to facilitate Guyana falling back on marked racial boundaries and geographical boundaries. Because of the tension of the time in the 1960's - people who lived in mixed communities, and were a minority, were forced to leave those communities and move back to communities where their group happened to be a majority. And so we have, right along the coast, many, many villages where you had majority Indians minority Africans, majority Africans, minority Indians, and they were forced to exchange their houses and go to other areas. For instance Buxton on the East coast - although primarily Africans - had a number of Indians; and Allandale - next door - was predominantly Indian, with a very small minority of Africans, and during the tension, the Indians from Buxton had to move over to Allandale, while the Africans from Allandale moved over to Buxton.' [10]

Here the argument is that the level and intensity of inter-ethnic conflict was raised, particularly during the 1961 election campaign, where race and ideology both played a significant role. Ethnic groups became strongly aligned to political parties, and ethnic minorities in the villages were forced to uproot themselves and seek security within their own communal lines. A contributing factor in this escalation of hostility was the imposition of a system of proportional representation, which was a thinly veiled attempt to oust the Jagan government by reducing the advantage of Indian superiority of numbers.

When the British governors announced this move, Jagan mobilised his supporters, calling out his sugar workers (largely Indian) to a strike which had a crippling effect on the economy. Sugar planters employed non-unionised labour (inexperienced in agricultural work) mostly Africans from Georgetown. Many of them acted as vigilantes, terrorising the Indian workers who had started a passive resistance campaign, particularly on the estates in West Demerara.[11] Furthermore the police, mostly Africans, were seen to co-operate actively alongside the strike-breakers, occasionally using violent methods to disperse peaceful picketers. In one incident at the Leonora plantation, workers who had been laid off due to their industrial action staged a peaceful 'sit in' were seriously injured, and in the case of one woman, killed, as a non-striker drove a tractor through them. Inevitably there were retaliations, and the situation deteriorated into terrorist attacks, bombing, shootings, and ambushes with casualties on both sides and ammunition for the British to further delay independence under a Jagan government.

Also discounting any simple law of ethnic polarisation, there was a third source for the increasing violence. There is documented evidence which shows that much of the violence and hatred was instigated by foreign intervention. There was the clearly visible form of the British troops and the sweeping powers given to them to search and detain at the height of the moral panic over Communist infiltration. A statement made by Arthur Schlesinger Jr. a political aide to President Kennedy, candidly spelled out the general intention of the British and Americans with regard to Guiana's future:

'As I reported to the President, an independent British Guiana under Burnham (if Burnham can commit himself to a multi-racial policy) would cause us many fewer problems than an independent British Guiana under Jagan.' [12]

The CIA had some influence in bringing down the Jagan government[13] By channelling funds through American labour organisations, the CIA was able to sustain one of the longest general strikes in history (lasting 79 days) led by the Civil Service Association, an African dominated institution. This strike and the social upheaval it caused served to widen the rift between African and Indian and effectively destroyed Jagan's government. Speaking with Dr Jagan on this issue in 1991 it was clear that he viewed foreign intervention as a major, if not *the* major, cause of ethnic polarisation in Guyana

"What is the trouble here in Guyana? It's foreign intervention and if you don't deal with that question you can't understand the racial problem or how this society evolved.... American intervention was a dominant factor – not that they weren't influential in the 1953 cold war period, with McCarthyism etcetera - but the 1961-1964 period was more intense, you had strong anti-Cuban policies, the missile crisis, Bay of Pigs invasion and so on. So we became the victims of the cold war".[14]

PNC in power

Once in power the PNC took action which undoubtedly reflected their concerns with a large and largely adversarial Indian population. Because of the perceived power of Indian-Guyanese in agriculture, and especially the rice industry, the PNC leadership neglected these areas and concentrated instead on a drive for industrialisation. The PNC '... could find no way to develop agriculture without benefiting those whose political support they did not enjoy'.[15] Furthermore, as the PNC increasingly took control of the state sector, productivity declined; and more professional people left the country, leaving industry frequently in the hands of inexperienced party members. One example of this dramatic decline was the newly nationalised GUYBAU (the renamed DEMBA project) bauxite mining project in Linden. Production of ore fell from 3.lm tons to 2.7m tons in 1970, and has declined ever since. Linden in the Nineties is a beaten destitute town, where the average miner's wage in 1991 was barely sufficient to survive on, and the PNC government of the day was considering selling half of the Linden operation to Alcan for a mere US$6 million.

The PNC declared itself a Marxist-Leninist party and used socialist rhetoric to rationalise the often punitive restrictions it imposed on the entire population. One example was the proclamation by Burnham that wheat flour would not be allowed into the country. Guyana did not produce wheat, so wheat was - for a time - categorised as an *'imperialist'* crop. Several Guyanese spoke with acrimony about the fact that an elite group was quite obviously benefiting from the privations suffered by the

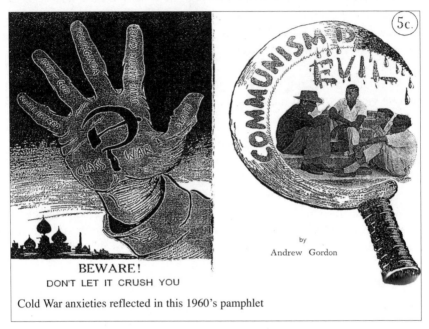

Cold War anxieties reflected in this 1960's pamphlet

ordinary citizen. Fancy goods and delicacies were confiscated on arrival at Timheri airport, yet imported luxury cars began to appear on the streets of Georgetown, and rumours abounded that much of the *'ideologically unsound'* food-stuffs ended up on the tables of PNC politicians and military groups.

The PNC's rigging of ballots was brought to international attention. Burnham was at pains to project an image of democracy, but the elections of 1968, 73, 78, 79, and 80 were denounced as fraudulent.[16] Once the basis for free and fair elections had been undermined, corruption could be seen to infest every area of public and private affairs in Guyana. The worsening of the economic situation was exacerbated by the IMF loans to Guyana. Professor Thomas sees this as a stage in the process of 'fascistisation' of the state. This is perhaps especially noticeable in Guyana, as the ruling class was able to gain power, bypassing the legitimate sanction of a popular social revolution, and actively undermining the electoral system. This manipulation of ideological power was accompanied by cuts in social services, increased taxes, and the removal of subsidies; in short the disappearance of anything but the facade of socialism.

Following this, there was a second stage characterised by a strengthening of the repressive forces of the state. By the late 1970's and early 1980's there was widespread use of repressive force in Guyana.

Industrial action was dealt with severely, and the judiciary was bent to the support of the executive arm of the state. As the climate of repression increased, opposition political groups formed and began to mobilise to defend democratic institutions. Now any pretence of representing a popular base disappeared and the third phase of the process occurred. This involved the direct attack on political opponents.[17] The rationalisation for acts of violence against opponents of the state was typically couched in terms of maintaining 'law and order' and 'we cannot afford the luxuries of democracy'.[18]

1964-1992

From the final collapse of Dr. Jagan's party in 1964 until October 1992, Forbes Burnham's People's National Congress held power in Guyana, initially in coalition with the United Force, led by Peter D'Aguiar, a businessman of Portuguese descent. It was a regime which ostensibly set out to empower the long repressed African-Guyanese (in Burnham's epithet *'to make the small man a real man'*) and, arguably, in the process, deprived the majority of urban African-Guyanese of a viable living. Two years after the PNC came into office the country finally achieved independence from Britain. The PPP having been removed from the political scene, Burnham had relative freedom to pursue his plans for the radical restructuring of the economy. The next steps

Forbes Burnham, Leader of the PNC

Burnham took were to break the monopoly of foreign ownership of Guyana's resources.

As a result of the swift nationalisation of 80% of the economy by 1977, all services in the country broke down. Grinding poverty became the norm for people who had enjoyed one of the most prosperous life styles in the Caribbean family of nations in which Guyana is usually placed. All commodity prices were inflated far in excess of public sector wage rises (approx. 300 to 400% compared to a rise of only 30 or 40% in pay rises). The government lost support on a massive scale.

Jobs in the expanded public sector went overwhelmingly to the African-Guyanese. The strength of PNC communal favouritism in both public and private spheres is clearly reflected in the African-Guyanese domination of public service, Defence Forces, mining, engineering and power production industries. This very blatant African-Guyanese bias greatly weakened the economy and the overall standard of living of all Guyanese.[19] Because of the perceived power of Indian-Guyanese in agriculture, and especially the rice industry, the PNC leadership neglected these areas, concentrating instead on a drive for industrialisation. The PNC '... could find no way to develop agriculture without benefiting those whose political support they did not enjoy'.[20]

The survival of the PNC as an elite regime produced the even more disastrous economic conditions which existed in the early 1990's, and there was a reduction in the society's ability to exercise control over the national economy. The most crippling manifestation of this was the acute foreign exchange crises which plagued all the territories.[21] Ten years on, the regime survived through the constant practice of rigging elections. There were further loans from the World Bank and the IMF, and the continued use of a system of patronage to ensure support from influential figures.

Since the death of Forbes Burnham in 1985, the regime softened its approach, and there was a marked decrease in the blatant violations of human rights. The regime survived by an increasingly elaborate matrix of controls, which are enshrined in legislation and major institutions in Guyana, and hence allowed the oligarchy to maintain dominance. Thomas claims that the regime '... gained full control of the state through a combination of communal politics and political patronage, racial support, patronage, and ideological acquiescence to powerful; international interests became the pillars upon which the regime developed and institutionalised its system of coercion and control'.[22]

Constitutional change

Throughout the 1970's and 1980's, the PNC attempted to increase its control over the state and its coercive institutions. By 1975, the party and the state were seen by many as virtually synonymous. The 1980 constitutional changes gave the president 'virtual imperial powers'. Article 182 of the constitution proclaimed that the president '... shall not be personally answerable to any court for the performance of the functions of his office or for any act done in the performance of those functions'.

The enemy was no longer one identifiable ethnic group, instead these sweeping powers were an indicator of the PNC regime's distance from any genuine electoral support. The regime had become an untouchable elite, with secret cadres and street forces which would neutralise any opposing voice. Yet as the economy declined and structure and order was eroded from the society, the PNC began to generate much broader and better organised opponents.

Resistance to the PNC

The sweeping powers the PNC conferred on itself, creating a virtual one party state, are perhaps in part a reaction to the fact that there was increasing multi-ethnic resistance to the party. This was of real concern to the regime.

Working People's Alliance which was formed in the mid 1970's, posed a real threat to the ruling party. The WPA advocated a multi-ethnic approach to government, recognising the contradictions and inherent instability of any one ethnic group holding the reigns of power. The WPA was founded by Walter Rodney, a Marxist historian and world renowned political activist. Rodney, being a true radical and an African-Guyanese, presented a strong challenge to the ruling African elite. The WPA garnered very strong support from all sections of the community and was able to '...organise and mobilise the entire spectrum of opposition forces, including Jagan's PPP, and unleashed a fierce assault on the government.' [23] This challenge struck at the heart of PNC support. It included mass rallies and industrial action, even in a place like Linden, the bauxite mining town long considered a PNC stronghold. Such threats from a multi-ethnic party (articulated by a black man) could not easily be deflected by appeals to communal solidarity, as when there was an identifiable ethnic enemy. In this way Jagan and other Indians had been dismissed as enemies stealing the country's wealth. Increasingly, the government began to resort to violence, intimidation and in some instances assassination of opponents.

There is little doubt that Rodney's own death was the direct result of a government campaign to silence its most serious critics. Premdas notes how the PNC '...appropriated the term 'terrorist' to describe the opposition' [24] and to rationalise their own tactics of political violence and arbitrary arrest of perceived enemies. George Lamming (the Barbadian poet) reflecting on Rodney's murder said '...no-one could recall, in the entire history of the country, so large and faithful a gathering assembled to reflect on the horror that had been inflicted on the nation. For Guyana had become a land of horrors.' [25] Having silenced the immediate threat from the WPA, the government went ahead with general elections. Despite national and international denunciations, the government awarded itself another two thirds majority, in an election which an international observer team described as 'rigged massively and flagrantly.' [26]

Walter Rodney

Tacit support for violence against Indians

The evidence of political terror and fraud used to defeat communal enemies seems indisputable. Although sporadic outbreaks of ethnic violence were not always orchestrated by the government, the government's failure to intervene can be seen as a form of complicity at the very least. The Wismar massacre of 24 May 1964, for example, was the culmination of several attacks and reprisals between Indians and Africans.[27] While the police and special volunteers looked on passively, the African-Guyanese engaged in an orgy of violence against the Indian community, involving rape, arson, beatings and murder.[28]

This is not to deny that there were atrocities committed by both sides. The present Post Master in Wismar, himself Indian, and several other local people, played the incident down claiming that it was in retaliation for the sinking of a boat, the Sun Chapman, which allegedly killed more than 20 African-Guyanese, a short time before. Nevertheless it seems that the government (if indeed not directly responsible for such acts) was reluctant to curb corrupt police and security forces that were able to rob and terrorise Indian citizens with little chance of reprimand or enquiry. Another source of fear and outrage, up to the present day, amongst Indians, was the alleged African theft of gold heirlooms and ornaments from Indians. Apart from setting up a climate of complicity, and not intervening to prevent acts of violence, like those at Wismar, there is strong evidence that Burnham used private death squads, provocateurs, and a variety of what Eusi Kwayana[29] called *'street-forces'*, to maintain consent and eliminate dissidents. Describing the change in the PNC's use of coercive force Kwayana said the following, "... The street thuggery is not present since about 1983 it began to crack up, even before Burnham died. The House of Israel, the street forces, the Young Socialist movement, and all the people like that, these were the street forces. The violence had run its course, it could achieve nothing more, and also these people, you know were well greased, there were all sorts of benefits they could receive. When the finances began to fail, they could not command the same presence on the streets." [30]

In the urban areas, especially Georgetown, the repression would become cross-cultural, but in the rural areas where Indians predominate, it would assume decided racist form. Rape, burglary, and arbitrary arrests by the security forces had become so prevalent that Indian villages became places of terror.[31] Frederick Kissoon, a columnist for the Catholic Standard, cited several examples of African-Guyanese police harassing only the Indian market traders:

'In one incident, the editor of this paper and I found ourselves at the Brickdam Police Station pleading for the release of a vendor who claimed that he was robbed by a policeman and when he accused his robber, he was in turn snatched away from his produce and taken to the station. The matter was later dropped by police. In the realm of traffic duties, a similar situation obtains; drivers are pulled over wrongfully and made to pay bribes.'[32]

Racism and election campaigns

It is significant that to speak of racism to many in Guyana is in itself considered racist and somewhat taboo. Eusi Kwayana made this point at an interview. He said that "...If you discuss racial problems you get the brand of being a racist, touching something which should not be touched. It is not a question which people discuss." [33] Yet, during party campaigning, there is much talk of the evils of racism, especially before an election. Each party makes a strong point of this stand. Premdas describes this process as, *'an obsessive ritual act'*, and regardless of the topic of his discussion, each speaker finds an opportunity to denounce Apanjaat (Hindi for literally *'vote race'*) politics. In all the available public media: pamphlets, radio broadcasts, newspaper advertisements racism is denounced by both parties.[34]

However, the ritual injunctions were very clearly not observed when it comes to *'informal'* campaigning. Premdas goes on to expose the *'unclean'* face of the campaigns in which grass-roots party workers used a variety of tactics to secure their respective ethnic voters. Commonly used were appeals to the old negative stereotypes which are ingrained in popular consciousness. Secondly, the campaigners made promises of preferential financial aid to either Africans or Indians. Indians are told flatly by PPP activists that when the PPP wins, the government will be *'ah'we government'* (our government). Indians are promised more land, higher prices for rice, and more government jobs. On the other hand, Africans are told just as brazenly that a PNC government will concentrate on urban needs such as housing and will expand the government to provide more jobs for Africans.[35]

The anger and suspicion which pre-election campaigning generated was apparent during the voter registration in April and May 1991. It was notable at the time that government officials who called on citizens to be enrolled on the electoral roll were chased away and in some instances beaten up.[36] Frederick Kissoon discussed this situation in his column in the radical newspaper, the Catholic Standard:

'A significant number of people are closing their doors to the enumerators, some are telling them they don't live there; some send out their children to say no one is at home. People have resigned a long time ago to the eternal rule of the PNC. If there is anything that people have come to believe is permanent, it is the unchanging rule of the PNC. They have seen four general elections and the country's only referendum reduced to a circus.'[37]

As Kissoon implies, there was a background of weary resignation regarding the political process. While these tactics in the *'unclean'* campaign are obviously not solely responsible for the existing animosity between the major groups, they must contribute to the level of tension in the community. Premdas makes a convincing case for the argument that '...in Guyana, competitive parties in quest of electoral votes deepen the divisions in the social system.'[38]

Guyana after Burnham

Some of the institutionalised means which the Burnham government had utilised to maintain power have, since his death from cancer in 1985, been removed. Desmond Hoyte who became the next President of Guyana made some significant concessions to reduce ethnic tensions in Guyana. These included abolishing the shady practice of the so called *'overseas vote'*, and cracking down on the use of the judiciary as an arm of the government to harass and prosecute political opponents.[39]

The possible political expediency of any improvements in the government's treatment of basic freedoms in Guyana is spelt out in the Guyana Human Rights Association's annual report 1990: 'An unavoidable conclusion to be drawn, despite improvements in the general level of respect, accorded to human rights in Guyana, is that respect for rights remains a matter of political convenience rather than institutional guarantee. All State institutions are vulnerable to political manipulation and abuse in a tradition buttressed by the supremacy of the ruling party. 'There is little evidence that institutions such as the judiciary, police force, and bodies such as the Elections Commission are able to withstand pressures which may be brought to bear on them to promote the government's party political interests'.[40]

The evidence clearly indicates that political campaigns and ethnic leadership have had a significant impact on inter-ethnic conflict in Guyana. Violence is meted out in real or symbolic form, and traditional stereotypes stemming from colonial days have been re-invoked in the drive for political power.

Furthermore, habitual repression and subversion of the constitutional process on the part of the PNC has led to the development of negative dispositions by both African and Indian-Guyanese cultures. However, change did occur largely due to external factors. Pressure from global financial structures (and the presence of many international observers) allowed the country to have the first free and fair elections in twenty six years. Relinquishing power during the 1992 elections in October, the PNC has finally been made to yield to genuine public opinion. The pendulum swung back to the opposition forces led by Dr Jagan, but with the emphasis, at least ostensibly, on a multi-ethnic coalition.[41]

1992-2003

Jagan was sworn in as President on October 9, 1992, after twenty eight years as the leader of the opposition. The new PPP/Civic has been under fairly constant and severe pressure from the outset. Some feel that in the first vital two years back in office the party made a lacklustre start failing to appoint the dynamic, broad-based cabinet that had been hoped for, slowing down the drive for privatisation and investment which had gained momentum under Hoyte, and squandering the goodwill and optimism which the apparent restoration of democracy seemed to promise. Jagan had some achievements between 1992 and 1997 – certainly there seemed to be a more genuine desire for reconciliation and working towards a more united coalition concerned with reflecting Guyanese hopes for a stable social and economic future.[42]

Jagan died on March 6, 1997, and his wife Janet assumed the mantle of President in December 1997 after national elections in which her

party (PPP Civic) won a 55% majority. Despite claims of transparency and free and fair voting the PNC disputed the result (they achieved 40% of the vote) and alleged that the results were fraudulent. There were public displays of dissatisfaction and violence and damage to property. Indeed since 1997 the ruling party has come under a sustained attack, leading to levels of distrust and violence which threatened a return to the upheavals of the early 1960's.

Dr Jagan, PPP leader

The situation was considered so grave that CARICOM intervened sending in a high level team to mediate the impasse. This led to the establishment of the Herdmanston Accord (signed on 17th January 1998) which appeared to be a ground breaking agreement between both the PPP Civic and the PNC with the following 5 point plan:

1. The PPP Civic would reduce its term in office from 5 to 3 years.

2. The PNC would call off its protestors from the streets and take up seats in parliament.

3. Dialogue would begin between the two major parties.

4. An audit would be carried out of the 1997 elections

5. There would be constitutional reform[43]

The agreement was further ratified at the St Lucia Summit in July 1998. Janet Jagan resigned in August 1999 due to ill health and was succeeded by Bharrat Jagdeo (who had been named as Prime Minister just a day earlier).

These attempts at some form of rapprochement between the two parties continued with a supposedly historic Dialogue or Communiqué between the Leader of the PNC/R (R standing for Reform) Desmond Hoyte* and the President Bharrat Jagdeo (PPP/Civic) on April 17th 2001

However, there is some concern that the conciliatory spirit of the PPP/C government was extracted by threats of disorder and violence against Indians, allegedly orchestrated by the PNC/R.

'...the Dialogue began on April 17, or thereabouts, less than 14 days after the President announced publicly that his administration would not talk under threats. In fact, speaking of threats, the very first two meetings occurred while violent acts were still being carried out against Indians by PNC supporters. Threat was always in the air (and still is); PNC supporters were outside the President's Office chanting, "No talk, more fire" as the two leaders talked.' [44]

In April 2003 the new PNC/R leader Robert Corbin vowed to thwart the Jagdeo government's

'... intention to move ahead on its own with the establishment of the four service commissions which have been held up for more than a year because of a stalemate between the ruling party and the opposition. The Public Service, Teaching Service, Police and Judicial Service Commissions are vital for the appointment and disciplining of workers in the various public sectors.' [45]

These service areas are all traditionally dominated by African-Guyanese workers, so Corbin's reaction seems somewhat predictable. Any attempt by an Indian-based government to extend authority over these areas would seem a direct threat - an attack on one of the few remaining areas of African-Guyanese pride.

Yet another attempt at dialogue took place between Robert Corbin the and President Jagdeo, this Communique of May 6, 2003 was, again, heralded as a breakthrough in the impasse and one that would allow for some measure of reasoned power sharing and open up a new era of *Constructive Engagement'* between the major political parties beneficial for the long-term social, economic and political development of Guyana. However, as before, such attempted accords have been criticised by groups on both sides of the ethno-political divide. Some Indians see the PPP/C as weak willed - being pushed around by the PNC/R and the threat of street violence and making major concessions (e.g. reducing terms of office from 5 to 3 years). Conversely any delay in implementation is seen as further proof of bad faith on the part of the PNC/R leadership. It appears that the manifestation of negative stereotypes (as discussed in detail in Chapter 2) is a constant feature of Guyanese social relations; on the one hand the Indian's fear of violence and personal attacks, on the other African mistrust of Indian manipulativeness.

There is evidence that implementation of the most recent pact has not been happening to plan. Corbin himself, in an Address to the Nation, implied that the PPP/C leadership had no intention of honouring the agreement. The troubled and complex issues of the political arena are especially exacerbated by – and reflected in – patterns of violent crime.

Current crime patterns

The linking of crime to race is a well established practice in Guyana. There has recently been a *'moral panic'* about a crime wave in Guyana. In February 2003 there was a much publicized jailbreak which left about 40 dangerous criminals at liberty (although at least 30 of these were killed or recaptured). Furthermore with the release of evidence by police of figures claiming 9 out of 11 crimes being committed by African-Guyanese men against *'selected'* Indian-Guyanese targets, there has been a sense of outrage and suspicion that the PNC may be coordinating a terror campaign against Indians.

'…in June 2001, the police issued a release stating to the effect that some clear patterns were visible from crimes being committed around that time—Indians were "selected" targets and 9 out of the 11 crimes tabulated, were committed by "Afro Guyanese men." While PNC leader, Mr. Hoyte, criticized the release as an "irresponsible" act, the PPP did not dispute it.'[46]

Several recent articles on the Guyana Under Siege website have included alarmist statements about the threat of rape and murder, and included tabloid style photographs of victims and survivors.

What you should expect, prepare yourself psychologically for, is the assaulting of our mothers and wives and sisters and daughters. Pray that these new bandits do not develop a taste for virgins, because they will not threaten to rape our 11-year-olds. They WILL rape them.[47]

However the actual figures for crime in Guyana are still relatively understated compared to most other countries in the region.

Others have called for a degree of caution and critical distance to be used – and to avoid reflex reaction of attributing all crimes by African-Guyanese against Indian-Guyanese as simply racially motivated. It must be remembered that while the figures may show a trend of Indians being the main victims there could be other more obvious reasons rather than needing to assume some political racially inspired conspiracy. Surely when the majority of prosperous businesses could be considered to belong to Indian-Guyanese these would be the logical targets for crime.

OFFENCES	GUYANA	TRINIDAD & TOBAGO	JAMAICA
Murder	125	188	1,139
Sex Offence	233	697	1,286
Serious Assault	413	634	9.179
Theft (All Kinds)	6,803	12,573	6,536
Fraud	162	293	994
Drug Offence	766	485	9,075

(Interpol International Crime statistics – 2001) [48]

The degree of truly worrying violence being used could also be linked to the growing prevalence of drug trafficking and racketeering.

'If Guyanese believe that criminalization is limited to the racial scope and racial disposition of crime in Guyana, then they are allowing the current violent, cancerous organized criminalization to go unchecked. This all-pervasive criminalization is not tinged by race but by the self-perpetuating conspiracy that functions for profit and power, and that endeavours to obtain immunity from the law through fear, corruption, and murder. This is organized crime in action and it is only one of the many variables in the current crime-fighting equation'. [49]

Nevertheless there are some indications that a more sinister, politically and ethnically motivated group is operating in Guyana. The following article in the (usually independent-minded) Stabroek News has alarming implications:

'There is ample evidence now that there is in existence a group of African Guyanese militants who are conducting an armed struggle. This group is not led or controlled by the People's National Congress (Messrs McAllister and Lowe had previously made this quite clear) but what Mr. Eusi Kwayana describes as the masterminds have some political connections. The group has reportedly lost faith in electoral democracy and feels oppressed by what they perceive to be economic victimisation and also by extra-judicial killings by a section of the police force...' [50]

In 2005 a book by Kean Gibson (an academic of Guyanese origins at the University of the West Indies in Barbados) highlighted a claim that African-Guyanese were being murdered as a result of racial abhorrence stemming from secret adherence to Hindu caste beliefs that African Guyanese were an unclean groups and an embodiment of evil which must be eradicated. Gibson suggests that such views were held at all levels within the PPP and had been acted upon with devastating results. That such a claim was not immediately ridiculed is indicative of the pernicious nature of ethnic politics. Hard evidence for these allegations appears to be virtually non-existent and the evidence which was presented could hardly be called rigorously researched, stemming, as it appears to, from statements made by callers to a reputedly hysterical chat radio show.

In fact the book has been condemned by the Ethnic Relations Commission (ERC) whose ruling noted:

'The Commission stresses that the author of the publication has advanced no facts whatsoever for the contention advanced that there exists an organized, systematic plan of oppression by Hindus/Indo-Guyanese of the Afro-Guyanese citizens of this country. Nor, in the public hearings undertaken by the Commission, was any evidence advanced to this effect, and the Commission is not otherwise aware of any evidence which would so suggest. The Commission emphasizes that the absence of such evidence in foundation of the thesis maintained by the author reduces the arguments advanced to mere hypothesis, supposition and opinion, unsubstantiated in fact and reality' (ERC Report, February 9, 2005).

However, the interesting point here is not the veracity of Gibson's claims but the reaction such a text has inspired. A number of African commentators seemed to be supporting Gibson's claims and scholarship, and even if they did not actively endorse the views they supported her right to express her views.

That murders of both African and Indian Guyanese have increased and reflect a new and callous brutality seems certain. However the spectre of secret political or religious cabals seems less likely to be the explanation. In a recent book *The Morning After* Eusi Kwayana has set out a different explanation which involves rival gangs and revenge slayings. However he raises the possibility that his analysis could be incorrect and that drugs trafficking could be part of the situation.

The political arena since 2000 then seems plagued by similar problems of stalled power sharing agreements, corruption and excesses in the justice and law enforcement system, evidence of organised crime, aggravated political demonstrations, inter-ethnic violence and possibly local politically affiliated terrorism.

NOTES AND REFERENCES

1   Mars, P, 1990
2   Premdas, R, 1986, p157
3   ibid
4   Jagan, C, 1984, p114
5   See anti-communist poster p.61

6   B.A.N, Collins in A, Rabushka, 1967, p102
7   Interview: University of Guyana, 9 April 1991
8   Jagan, C, 1998, 17
9   Mars, P, 1990, p4
10 Interview: Universtiy of Guyana, 11 April 1991
11 Jagan, C, 1997, p306
12 Schlesinger in Jagan, C, 1997, p378
13 Agee, P, 1975, p293; Sunday Times, 16 and 23 April 1967; 2001 Guyanaundersiege.com, Declassified Documents on British Guiana
14 Interview with Dr Jagan, 4th May, 1991
15 Latin American Bureau, 1984, p47
16 See Premdas, R, 1972, 1972b, 1986, 1987
17 Thomas, C, 1982, p15
18 ibid, p16
19 For statistics see the International Commission of Jurists, Geneva, 1965. See also Premdas, R, 1987
20 Latin American Bureau, 1984, p47
21 Thomas, C, 1982, p14
22 Thomas, C, 1982, p13
23 Premdas, 1987 , p34
24 ibid
25 Latin American Bureau, 1984, p80
26 Latin American Bureau, 1984, p81
27 C, Jagan, 1997, pp305-312.
28 Latin American Bureau, 1984 , p43
29 Charismatic leader of the WPA
30 Kwayana Interview, 18 April 1991
31 Premdas, R, 1987, p36
32 Catholic Standard, 31 March 1991, p7
33 Kwayana Interview, 18 April 1991
34 Premdas, R, 1972b, p287
35 Premdas, R, 1972b, p 292
36 Stabroek News, 12 April 1991
37 Catholic Standard, 21 April 1991
38 Premdas, R, 1972b , p274
39 Premdas, R, 1987
40 Guyana Human Rights Association, Guyana Human Rights Report, p2
41 See example of People's Coalition for Democracy handbill in Appendix, the slogan, 'join forces to keep hunger away' captures the mood of the time
42 See Stabroek Editorial – Nov 9, 2002: A Leap of Faith
43 Stabroek News, September 30th 2001 'Racial Divide Must be Bridged Now'
44 http://www.guyanaundersiege.com/Topical%20Affairs/Under%20the%20shadow%20of%20a%20gun.htm Rakesh Rampertab
*Desmond Hoytes died in 2002
45 Stabroek News April 4, 2003
46 http://www.guyanaundersiege.com/Security/Crime%20and%20Racism.htm by Rakesh Rampertab Dec 15, 2002
47 http://www.guyanaundersiege.com/Women/Defense%20of%20Our%20Women.htm sept 11, 2001 Rakesh Rampertab
48 http://www.gina.gov.gy/archive/releases/gr030806.html
49 ©2001-2003. Government Information Agency (GINA). Article Prem Misir, Ph.D. - Organized Crime, a most sinister kind of crime that is huge and growing.)
1 Stabroek News, November 5, 2002.

CHAPTER 4
Arenas of Cultural Struggle

The charade of ethnic harmony

In Georgetown, both African and Indian Guyanese have often to work and mix closely. It is an uncomfortable situation which requires stage management skills, but provides countless opportunities to both assert and resist dominant values. Guyana may be represented as an arena or a stage where the real enmities of ethnic division are stoically disguised. Many Africans and Indians may live in mixed neighbourhoods in towns or villages, their children attending the same schools under a racially integrated staff. According to Premdas, this '...overt inter-racial interaction is plentiful, easy to be interpreted as evidence of unity and harmony'.[1]

It is important here to reaffirm the essential difference between a private ethnicity and a public ethnicity, because it is within and between these different social zones, that the drama of ethnic identity and difference is played out. The private ethnicity is maintained primarily in the private domain of cultural life, that is in social activity associated with the family and home, affairs in the homeland, and with issues associated with the past. The public domain is maintained primarily '...in activities associated with schooling, employment, the laws of the state and general human services'.[2]

There seems to be the same tacit accord between the rival groups in the public domain, as occurs between the members of the crew on board a ship. In that situation as Erving Goffman and latterly Greg Dening[3] (1992) have shown us, because of the importance of a cohesive team, especially when the tasks are dangerous, aggression and conflict are deferred to the *'off stage'* periods of shore leave. Open acknowledgement of these feelings on board would make the limited territory available in which people must work side by side unbearable, and might be a potential threat to the safety and well-being of others. On the other hand, at times the stress caused by this charade can spill over into violent outbursts.

In Georgetown, a predominantly African town, the proximity of the *'other'* and the bitter memories of racial violence tend to preclude any overt public expression of ethnic antagonism, particularly amongst Indian-Guyanese who, despite their growing prominence in the professions, have traditionally been denied access to the higher levels of industry and commerce and frequently face discriminatory treatment from the African-Guyanese authorities. Indeed to openly question the divisions in Guyanese society or to discuss ethnic politics is to risk being branded as racist. Premdas has noted that in Guyana:

'Inter-racial suspicion runs silently deep, each side engaged in a contrived drama of studied hypocrisy about inter-communal amity. In the deepest recess of the soul runs a torrent of hate that makes everyday a veritable civil war, a struggle for ethnic ascendancy, a neurotic fear of ethnic domination, all enacted as an elaborate ritual of seeming routine and peace'.[4]

Despite a degree of hyperbole, which is perhaps a feature of some expatriate Guyanese, here is a taste of opposed ethnic energies beneath the exterior calm of Guyana. In such an atmosphere the self-conscious charade represents a use of diplomacy not only for survival but also as a means of undermining the other. Douglas talks of the '...social uses of the environment as a weapon of mutual coercion'.[5]

Cricket and the struggle for symbolic dominance

In Guyana, as in many plural societies, one form of establishing or attempting to establish hegemony is to deny the reality of ethnic inequality and division and to attempt to instil Guyanese identity among all Guyanese. During my visit in 1991, this was clearly the official line presented by PNC spokespersons. Questions of political and economic polarity along ethnic lines are avoided and the broader ethnic composition of Guyana is emphasised as in the cliché of 'Guyana - the land of six peoples', a multicultural society in which all ethnic groups are recognised and accorded equal status'. But social interaction in everyday public life is frequently a battleground for symbolic domination and resistance to that domination. Sport is one facet of social life which highlights the *'embarrassing'* disparities between the status of the two groups and the strategies the disadvantaged group employs to *'save face'*.

Cricket has been an important symbolic field amongst people in the Caribbean. Several writers have recognised its special significance. St Pierre described cricket as an arena for acting out many of the frustrations implicit in a colonial people. It has been described as a 'mass therapy for West Indians'. Cricket, '...operates as a leveller of differences in West Indian society. The game has succeeded in removing the ascriptive basis (e.g. on colour and race) for ranking individuals in society and replacing it with as achievement oriented basis'. (e.g. merit and ability)[6]

Rodney talks of cricket as one example of the colonial hegemony which both groups have taken up:

'Both major racial groups responded in like manner to certain aspects of the culture of the dominant Europeans: notably, to the game of cricket and to the institution of the rum shop'. [7]

The game has allowed expressions of national pride and resistance and certainly was one aspect of colonial life, along with the rum shop, which was taken up wholeheartedly by both Afro and Indo-Guyanese. It also contributed to the process of *'Creolisation'*.

Frank Birbalsingh claims that cricket serves a similar function in Guyana to the bull fight in Spain. It is '...a spectacle that can galvanise people's spiritual resources, stimulate their national self esteem, remind them of their place in the world'.[8] This is not a way of demeaning West Indian people or under-playing their achievements in many other areas, or of denying their abilities in improving quality of life through progressive action in the region. Indeed, it '...recognises West Indian resistance to an oppressive colonial legacy; for it acknowledges test cricket as the first opportunity that West Indians had of demonstrating their abilities on the international scene'. [9]

While it is certainly true then, that cricket gave countries like Trinidad and Guyana international recognition and a sense of national pride, it was not until 1950 that a West Indian cricket team included an Indian. Birbalsingh explains this late entry to the sport as a result of '...the undisputed dominance of Creoles before and after colonial times, and that being bonded to the plantation system Indians would not have been encouraged to get involved'.[10]

David Dabydeen, a Guyanese poet shows in a poem from his *Coolie Odyssey* the sustaining power which Indian players provided for the Indian-Guyanese community, particularly at the time of the 1962 – 64 violence. In the poem quoted below he refers to the incident at Wismar where a number of Indians were killed and Indian women raped by an organised party of African-Guyanese (often claimed as retaliation for the suspected sinking of a ferry boat by Indians on which twenty six African-Guyanese died).

For Rohan Bholalall Kanhai

1.
Kanhai
Cutlass whack six
Leather ball red
Like Whiteman restless eye
One ton cane - runs
Cropped all day in hot sun the man cut and drop on he back
To hook two and lash four.
Hear the Coolies crying out for more!
England glad bad when clouds
Puff and scowl and blue
Like end-of-over-bowlerman
And day done in rainburst:
God is white Overseer for true!

2.
And when darkness break and Blackman buss we head Wismar-side and bleed up we women
And Burnham blow down we house and pen Like fire-ball and hurricane
And riverboat pack with crying and dead Like Old Days come back of lash and chain Is round the radio we huddle to catch news of Kanhai batting lonely in some far country Call Warwick-Shire, and every ball blast is cuff he cuffing back for we,

Driving sorrow to the boundary
Every block-stroke is paling in a fence He putting down to guard we,
And when century come up, is like dawn.

Missie and the Coconut Man: Toolsie's Task

Coconut gripped in outstretched hand
Ready to pelt like cricket ball,
Two twitches of his cutlass, preparatory
Batsman tapping at the crease,
Then downward swoop of blade
Hard, straight, unequivocal-
And head chop clean off
Boss bowler blasting away the bail

Or spinning the thing in his palm
Chipping here and there
Shaving and shaping a pleasing mouth,

Cutlass crafting victory
The cunning of a coolie Ramadhin
Whilst Missie waits indifferent to
The fantasy
Fingering her riding whip impatiently.

(From Coolie Odyssey, Hansib 1988)[11]

In these poems Dabydeen uses the metaphor of cricket to explore the relationship of power and resistance, and the continuous link in the chain of oppression, at the hands of both Whiteman and Blackman. The labour in the cane fields is etched into the Indian personality and resonates with the stroke of the cricket bat. There is here the sense of the habitus, the deep-seated and ingrained effect of practices shaping a people and sustain them against the culture of the *'other'*. The use of colloquial Creolese gives the poems a dialectic energy plain English would not possess. *'Lash'* and *'cuff'* provide directness and a connection between tools of labour, exploitation and recreation: the cutlass which cuts the cane, the whip which was used to flog plantation workers, and the cricket bat which here transmutes the strokes of the latter into a symbol of the resistance of Indians to oppression.

The rhythm and pattern of these expressions show clearly the depth conditioned and formative nature of the habitus. Cricket as a colonial practice is clearly part of a deeply influential system of meaning.

Yet, though cricket is a colonial legacy shared by both African and Indian-Guyanese alike, the fact that African-Guyanese dominate the present West Indies team, is seen by Indians as a further attempt to remove Indians from public life (in just the same way they claim they have been denied access to the public service and of course, during the 28 year of PNC rule, the political arena).

Cricket highlights the inherent inequalities and rivalries between the two groups, even though its attractiveness to both groups arises from a common colonial experience; cricket – then - is also an illustration of a shared habitus which exists across ethnic lines. The poems are more than just a further chapter in the *Coolie Odyssey*, a chronicle of Indian endurance in the face of continued oppression. They are redolent of a shared Guyanese culture. The images of slavery and plantation work or the work of a street vendor are also very much part of African-Guyanese social values. The idea of a shared creole habitus shaped through the physical and mental rigours of work is transmuted into the actions of cricketers, and provides salvation in the face of degradation and repression for Africans as well as Indians in Guyana. This sort of transmutation is achieved not just by poets but is there to be observed in everyday life in Guyana.

However, as a field of symbolic dominance, cricket has at times been seen by Indians, in my observations in the 1990's for example, as a display of excess in which their absence was yet another reminder of their loss of political power. It is when such overt displays of dominance occur that the reality of ethnic division is revealed. Perhaps before the advent of the PNC and the subsequent disadvantages that Indians in Guyana found themselves labouring under, the ethnic composition of the West Indies team would not have been such an issue.

Frederick Kissoon in a 1991 article 'Cricket, racialism and Guyana's future',[12] explains the behaviour of Indian cricket spectators, which scandalised many Guyanese, in the following manner.

'What happens over a long period of time, in a small society like Guyana, is that the discriminated section becomes psychologically insecure and harbours deep resentment against those who they feel are responsible for this state of affairs. This resentment operates at two levels; one in which the group comes to identify all members of that predominant section as privileged ones in the society, rather than focusing their bitterness only on the ruling politicians. Secondly, the psychological insecurity is allowed an escape mechanism:

When any and everything the favoured group does fails, the discriminated section applauds. By doing so this section feels a small victory is achieved against those who deny them opportunities and oppress them'.[13]

Popular visions of ethnic conflict

During my brief visit to Guyana I had the privilege to meet with Martin Carter perhaps Guyana's greatest poet. Carter's vision of an ethnic difference and unreasoning violence is captured in this anecdote he related to me (Martin died in 1997).

Mr Carter beckoned me into a spacious front room adorned with Amerindian artifacts, and other inspiring things. Martin Carter projects largesse, an immediate compassion and seriousness within a frame of gentleness, civility and modesty edged with a certain shambling grittiness.

MC: "When a crisis comes – belonging to a different race becomes a resource. So I am making the two terms *'crisis'* and *'resource'*. That is to say that when something happens that an individual of one racial group cannot cope with – he regresses towards his racial stock – as a resource, as a vision to help him'

SS: "So the crudest stereotypes emerge"

MC: "and dreadful things will be said.."

SS: "I am hearing this everyday when people start talking in taxis –terrible tirade of abuse"

MC: "You make a very sharp observation about the taxi. For instance in a taxi you may not see it too easily, but it happens. Let us assume that the taxi driver is a man of Indian descent. There is a tendency for him to ignore the person who is of African descent and vice versa. So that would therefore mean that the people in a taxi would more likely be of one group – and so again you will get what you just described – like-minded people you see, who are really reinforcing their perceptions. And it is worse now, it never used to be like that until ten years ago… but in the debasement it has now become a sort of protest against … and it can get ugly - at least verbally.

As I said when it becomes a critical imbalance – and I've seen this in '62' and the dimensions of it are horrendous.

I'll give you an example and one which sticks in the mind. In 1962 this very street – not here - but further up, in which a man, a young man, riding his bicycle, he's wearing a hat, so his head is covered (and in those days people attacked one another, especially if they were in a disadvantaged situation). So this young man came along, and some young dark boys came out of a shop or something and attacked him, started belabouring him with sticks. Now the young man who is riding the bicycle realises what is going on very clearly, because he lives here – and the problem was that he was normal dark brown, but his features were more aquiline than average. So he instinctively realised that these chaps had attacked him because of his apparent resemblance to an East Indian. Realising this he tore the hat off his head - and said to them 'What you beating me for? Look at my hair' (for he had negro-type hair). And then when they paused – only momentarily – he said in explanation, 'My mother was an Indian and my father was a blackman.' And the reply was as follows, which is the real horror, they said: 'Oh so your mother was an Indian and your father was a blackman – well we beat the East Indian within you.'

When you reach that state of irrationality you understand that is why I say it is a resource. That has gone beyond politics, its no longer a disagreement with a party, it's now become existential – in the worse sense of the word."

(in Spencer (2006 – 169-70) from interview recorded in Georgetown April 1991)

Later that month I spoke to Paul O'Hara[14] who recounted a similar story. His rendition was more of an anecdotal thing (he described racism in Guyana as like a "comic strip thing"). He also described an incident from 1962 in which a doogla[15] person was beaten – first by some Indians and then by some Africans. "We're going to beat this out of him and then we're going to beat that out of him..."

These stories which have the same narrative structure indicate the ambivalence both major ethnic groups have to the idea of *'mixed'* identity, but also perhaps indicates the deep-seated anxieties that the incidents in 1962 have left on the collective psyche of the Guyanese.

Martin Carter, Guyana's most famous poet who died in 1997

PNC's loss of ideological dominance

Since independence, the PNC has lost its ability to effectively attain ideological domination, and has become increasingly dependent on coercive means. If, as a theory of practice suggests, '...those leaders will succeed whose personal identity myths resonate with evolving configurations of habitus, practice, and experience',[16] then it seems that the ruling elite in 1991 had come to a critical juncture. The regime was no longer able to address an ethnic constituency, which could be depended upon, even to maintain *'face'*, let alone the semblance of legitimate government. Instead, the governing elite became further removed from the impoverished citizens it purported to represent. The regime has consequently lost its ability to produce discourse, which appropriates the experience of many Guyanese, or even that of the African-Guyanese from whom it derived its original support. This failure of symbolic domination is not necessarily recognised overtly given that '... domination operates through the habitus and cannot be apprehended consciously, breakdowns in regimes of domination (like their operation) cannot be recognised as such. Instead they are likely to be experience indirectly, often as crises of ethnic identity'. (ibid:43)

In Guyana these signs of crisis are most apparent in the plight of the African-Guyanese. Empowered by the early PNC years and the vision of Burnham, many Africans were led to believe that independence under Burnham's PNC would unlock the country's wealth and finally recognise the years of hardship and degradation, affirming the Africans' rightful place as the true heirs and shapers of Guyana.

It is a potent myth and one echoed by other revolutionary movements at the time, in Africa especially. Yet the very regime which held such glittering prizes before their eyes, was quickly to prove yet another link in the chain of oppression. The result has been that many urban Africans have suffered a further blow to their sense of self-esteem and experienced insecurity and confusion of identity. Dr Jagan expressed the contradictory position of the African-Guyanese under PNC rule in the following manner:

'...we don't describe this government as a black government we say it's got a dual tendency - that is in relation to other races it is black, but at the same time its anti -working class, and the majority of the blacks are working people therefore it's against black people'.[17]

On the other hand, the identity and position of many Indians, while living in comparable poverty, was more securely anchored to religious and cultural traditions. But for African-Guyanese, the new state had to succeed in regaining a sense of pride and achievement.

The PNC regime after Burnham recognised the need to remove the emphasis on ethnicity, to establish domination which did not limit them to a narrow part of the ideological field. When more than 50% of the population are of a different ethnic background, the pro-African rhetoric and revolutionary fervour was undoubtedly of limited value. This is particularly the case when the majority of African-Guyanese workers, as state employees, were suffering from the government's repressive and dictatorial labour laws, and the impossibility of living on the wages of a public sector employee.

Formation of distinct yet overlapping ethnic habitus

We have seen the stage-managing of everyday social encounters between the two groups. Such encounters are stage managed to project an image of public harmony - and to allow the necessary exchanges of everyday life. But this public stage management, in which both ethnic groups collaborate, is a thin and brittle veneer over a deeply divided society. There was a struggle for symbolic domination pursued by the ruling party; an attempt to construct homogeneity of ethnic values, which has been roundly resisted and scorned by Indian citizens. Despite the apparent depth of the gulf separating the two ethnic groups, there is evidence of unity based on the shared experience of hardship, an experience which has, ironically, brought forward shared meanings and dispositions from the two ethnic habitus. The PNC's attempt to maintain hegemony was resoundingly rejected under the country's first free and fair elections when in 1992 the opposition parties in coalition won a landslide victory. Rather than a repressive state imposing a dominant ideology on ethnic groups which passively accept it, there has been active negotiation and confrontation in the construction of ethnic boundaries. The Guyanese citizen - Indian or African appears to be an active agent in the construction of distinct but overlapping ethnic habitus.

NOTES AND REFERENCES

1   Premdas, R, 1992, pp1-2.

2   Turpin, T, 1990, p6.

3   Dening, G, 1992

4   Premdas, R, 1992, p3.

5   Douglas, M, 1975, p5.

6   Caribbean Quarterly, 1973, p26.

7   Rodney, W, 1981, p179.

8   Dabydeen, D, 1987, p265.

9   ibid

10 ibid

11 Dabydeen, D, 1988

12 Catholic Standard, 31 March 1991.

13 Catholic Standard, 31 March 1991.

14 Paul O'Hara – was a senior journalist for the PNC newspaper The Chronicle

15 'dougla' – is a person of mixed African and Indian origin

16 Bentley, C. 1987, p47.

17 Interview, 4 May 1991.

CHAPTER 5
The outlook for the future

Crossing boundaries

This section will examine cases of boundary crossing and trace the extent to which the individual is able to play and negotiate the markers of ethnic identity. Conversely, the extent to which ethnic categories are still firmly imposed, consolidated and reproduced in Guyanese culture will be noted.

Williams[1] suggests that the typical Guyanese person is constantly evaluating members of other groups by means of an internalised hierarchy of *'givers and takers'* (see Appendix 1). These are categories which are based on generalised racial and cultural strata purporting to reflect relative contributions to the society. The hierarchy imposed in colonial times positioned the English and other Europeans at the top. Next the pale-skinned Chinese, and beneath them the Portuguese (who were not recognised as Europeans). Then Indians, next the Africans, and at the bottom of the pyramid the indigenous Amerindians (who could not be successfully pressed into plantation labour and were consequently considered useless). The hierarchy was based on a colour code and a perception of cultural advancement (with English values enshrined as the yardstick by which all others were judged).

This code was challenged during the second half of the Twentieth Century. Africans and Indians, low in the colonial hierarchy, vie to have their contribution to Guyanese development and their distinctive qualities recognised as legitimating a position at the top of the post colonial status hierarchy. Beneath them are the Chinese (who are so well integrated that they are barely visible as a separate minority) the Portuguese (a group of negligible size) and then the American Indians (regarded as a servant class when urban), and beneath them the English and other Europeans (although this reversal belies the lingering affinity for English values espoused by some Guyanese). The weapons in the battle over status supremacy are the stereotyped views of the other - stereotypes which, as we have seen, were initially assigned to the ethnic groups by the colonial rulers and adopted by the opposed ethnic groups in colonial times.

It has been argued that under colonial rule subordinated ethnic segments '...accepted Euro-cultural domination in practice and utilised racial stereotypes derived from this elite stratum to compete for and justify their rights to certain economic and political benefits'.[2] Stereotypes, derived from colonial values, were formative in defining ethnic identity and drawing ethnic boundaries. Yet despite the tendency to view fellow Guyanese as competitors for power and resources based on a perception of their relative efforts in building the society, we have seen that, as Williams argues, a contradictory democratic notion exists. This is the notion that every Guyanese has some mixed blood, such that racially-based ascriptions are unfounded. Many Guyanese realise that the only future for Guyana is one which is built from the diversity of all groups.

This ambivalent attitude of some Guyanese may be occasionally expressed - even to an outsider - as a grudging respect for the other group. Fieldwork examples illustrate the manner in which each group speaks about the other. Subjects accepted some of the negative values assigned to their ethnic group, and expressed admiration for aspects of the other group's culture. Louis, an African-Guyanese surveyor, resident of Buxton, made the following comments:

"The Indian element in the community have more of a communal approach to a problem. They would normally perform a service which could be beneficial to the entire community, Now the negro is so factionalized that anything you try to attempt for them, is being defeated, or someone find a better argument - and the community seem to lack the progressive stress .... we so factionalized we find it difficult to communicate with each other because someone come with idea - you wanna be smart - you wanna play dis - you wanna play dat - you know... It become so individualistic...we cannot get them to come together en masse and say we're going to do this ... Even if say this is so - some individual will come and factionalize it. They can sway so fast and break up so fast it amaze me". (Interview extract 11/4/1991)

So it seems that some professional African-Guyanese, typified by Louis, were well able to accept criticism about other African-Guyanese and (at least part of the time) to attribute important and positive traits to the Indian-Guyanese. Louis continued:

"In the Indian you don't find that - they just harmonious blending of the personality - of the soul, of the spirit of these people - and you have to give them credit for that ... The priest and the pandit have done a wonderful job in the social sphere".

Louis conceded what he called 'flaws in the Negro system of survival of the community' and, by contrast, spoke with respect about the harmony and co-operation within the Indian community. Yet not long afterwards he became less complimentary and indignant when the question of Indian land ownership came up.

"Every one of dem got two tractors - got the combining tractors and large, houses, and still own the land. They can afford to carry on planting because they have money in the bank. These same people - they can go up to the States - maybe twice a year - I can't even go - as a public servant and take a holiday here in Bartica". (Interview Buxton, 11/4/91)

From similar conversations with both African and Indian-Guyanese it seems that there are frequently contradictory elements in each group's expression of the *'other'*. Individuals, assessing individuals from another ethnic group, will often draw on universal Guyanese criteria rather than ethnic stereotypes. In the presence of an outside observer, at least, many Guyanese refuse to discuss issues of ethnic identity maintaining that the issue would involve them in racist behaviour. However, as in the case of Louis, the application of universal criteria and a public rejection of racist discourse will alternate with reversion to stereotypical categorization of the other. The trigger for reversion, in this case is resentful reflection on economic difference: the ready explanation for hurtful inequality appears to lie in the old stereotypes of the ethnic other. In the case of Louis, the reversion is to the ethnic stereotypes about Indian acquisitiveness and wealth, with the sense of betrayal and injustice implicit in them.

An example of an Indian-Guyanese who expressed a similarly ambivalent attitude to African-Guyanese culture was provided by Anna, a teenager from a modern Muslim family just outside Georgetown. Her family were relatively wealthy shop-keepers and merchants in Chateau Margot. She quite openly expressed her disdain for things Indian and her appreciation of and attraction to African culture, particularly musical trends, (especially reggae), dance styles, and a perceived image of Africans as being less hide-bound and ritualistic, and more free to express themselves. This seemed to stem partly from her isolation at a predominantly African school and the routine ragging she received as a *'coolie girl'*.

Yet despite these signs of interest in African culture and her strident disregard for her own ethnic parentage, she was repelled by and derisive of people with a darker skin. This was illustrated by her relations with an uncle Asiz. Asiz was very dark skinned, possibly of Tamil origin, and during the playful taunting she received from him she retorted by calling him *'blackman'*, quite a strong term of abuse , forgiven only because of their role as close kin and sparring partners, which made the exchange almost stylised.

B.F. Williams, through her study of Cockalorum, a village of East Coast Demerara, shows how contradictory methods of evaluating the other are systematised. She noted the concern of villagers with developing criteria to determine a just system of political participation, and distribution of economic benefits and responsibilities. She noted that subjects frequently draw upon *'contradictory sets of ideological precepts'*, egalitarianism and hierarchy. Egalitarianism reflects the popular belief that Guyanese of all ethnic origins have made and continue to make significant contributions to the nation, and contend that *'Awl ahwee a Doogla'*. (everyone is a Doogla, i.e. of mixed race)[3] Hierarchy - as we have seen - reaffirms the relative positions of the ethnic groups in a power structure.

This intense awareness of ethnic hierarchy was highlighted in the following anecdote related by a Guyanese anthropologist, Dennis Bassier. In his student days, he told me, an African girl became attracted to him. The manner in which their relationship developed highlights the intense awareness of ethnic difference but also the fact that such differences can be negotiated and overcome:

"Umm 1 was a student here in the early 1970's and there was a black girl who would sit in class with me and so on. And she became attracted to me, but her orientation was so strong - that she could not accept that she was falling for an Indian - and she looked at me and said: 'You know you're not Indian.' I said 'Yes I am Indian.' She said, 'Oh no no your hair is kinda curly, wavy when it's long.' And I said, 'No Indians do have wavy hair - look at the Madrasees, for instance , the Dravidians?' She said 'Ah no no - do you eat roti in the morning?' (Now this is Indian food) I said "No most mornings 1 eat bread, crackers what have you." She said "Oh Ok then you're not Indian.' She said 'When you eat, before you eat do you feed your dog or cat?' (And this is true this is very very marked among Indians - they would take a little of their food and give it to the dog or cat before they eat themselves.) I said, 'No I don't, whatever is left I give.' 'Oh then you're not Indian - all Indians do that ... (laughs) So what I say is it comes back to the stereotypes we have of these categories ... and since I don't do those two things among the others then, OK I feel satisfied to myself that this man is not Indian so I can go ahead', (laughs)." (Interview at University of Guyana 9/4/1991)

In this instance, the two forces, egalitarianism in recognition of the Indian as desirable, and hierarchy in the recital of markers of ethnic status, seem to be the site of an individual struggle to transcend prescribed boundaries.

What is extraordinary here is first - that the young African-Guyanese woman should feel it necessary to put the object of her affections through this test when it seems unlikely that, at least on surface appearance, there could have been any mistaking his *'Indianess'*. Second the recital of cultural markers is surprising in that it seems so fluent and detailed an inventory that, had even these been thwarted, one imagines she would have been able to continue the litany of distinctive features until she struck one which would have achieved the desired result. This aspect of boundary crossing points to the possibility that subjects are not constrained by any simple determinism, and they may be knowledgeable and able to consciously manipulate elements in the social world.

This may mark a point of departure from Bourdieu who presents practice as the product of processes which are an unconscious (or not fully conscious) understanding of the social world - which begins in childhood - and which gives the actor an implicit understanding of what is the right action to take. The criticism that Bourdieu's work is unable to account for individual subjectivity, and the contention that individuals are more conscious of the social world than Bourdieu is prepared to allow is raised in Jenkins' critique of Bourdieu:

'the role in social life of deliberate, knowing, decision making, informed by whatever rationality is the order of the day, is vastly under-estimated by Bourdieu ... Bourdieu's refusal to accept this leads him inexorably into deterministic explanations.' (1992:97)

The woman in this example is certainly very *'knowing'* and deliberate in her use of these symbolic codes, these elements of habitual behaviour, and is consciously using this knowledge to cross a cultural boundary. It seems more than likely that Indian-Guyanese faced with a similar dilemma might equally use knowledge of social categories in a functional manner to achieve a desired result.

However the incident described above does reaffirm Bourdieu's view of symbolic domination. The fact that such exchanges are necessary is in itself somewhere at the back of their minds, of the evidence that both parties have what Bourdieu calls 'the feel for the game' a second nature instilled in them from childhood. And certainly this second nature is not fully conscious.

It is the social actors understanding 'albeit usual pattern of how things are done or happen' (Jenkins, 1992: 72)

Such exchanges are examples of boundary crossing, but the individual's behaviour is ironically expressing the power of the symbolic codes and dispositions which are generated by the Indian and African habitus. So in this interpretation, Bourdieu's view of practice appears not overly deterministic; rather the analogy to language or other symbolic codes is highlighted. The fact that the two students had to go through a stylised ritual in order to express their attraction to one another shows the implicit nature of the social codes which define ethnic groups. Yet it also demonstrates the strategic use of codes in a knowing and conscious manner, with results which might take the actors outside of the accepted norms for their respective ethnic groups.

While Bourdieu's theory certainly suggests that there are recognised rules by which social actors communicate across social divides. This example shows a conscious and playful manipulation of these boundary markers rather than the blind determination of unconscious conditioning.

The African and Indian habitus are produced by (and in turn generate) contradictory dispositions. Ethnic identity is a complex negotiation between the public and the private, the hierarchical and the egalitarian, the individual and the societal. There is a historical solidarity between the African and Indian in Guyana, stemming from their similar treatment as the vassals of an exploitative colonial society. Yet these common experiences, which have developed something like a Creole habitus, have also sowed the seeds of inter-ethnic rivalry and separatism.

This ambiguous legacy of common experiences has variously provided a base for relations of competition or collaboration at each shift in economic and political power. Brackette Williams has, more than any other contemporary observer of Guyana, successfully described the process of the evolution of new cultural nationalisms in Guyana and negotiations between them. The withdrawal of colonial powers set in motion the struggle between the two major ethnic blocs and their distinct cultural nationalisms. Williams sets out the dynamics of this process, and anticipates the following.

'The outcome of this process depends on a change in the form of hegemony out of which these cultural nationalisms were produced and commitments to them ingrained in the collective meanings of local communities. It is not a matter of time, proximity, the permeability of ethnic boundaries, or other forms of cultural interchange per se. For nearly two decades now physical representatives of the Anglo-European elite that fostered a particular transformist hegemony have been numerically insignificant, but the constraints this kind of hegemony implied remain.' 6

The persistence of colonialist values has been evidenced earlier in this book. The imposed functional constraints of an aggressive colonial power with a belief in a hierarchy of racial, moral and cultural superiority, on which they positioned themselves at the apex. This internalised hierarchy distorts identity of the colonial subject leading some to aspire and emulate the same imposed values which degrade and exploit.

'These constraints continue to set the coordinates of the ideological field in which, Guyanese seek to reassess previous standards of civilised conduct and to homogenise contemporary heterogeneity. They move back and forth between hierarchical and egalitarian precepts, while maintaining the centrality of contribution and place as key sources of criteria against which to evaluate elements of heterogeneity and the potential each element has to serve as a feature of a new standard of civilisation.' 7

The future

Williams has argued that this dynamic process may finally stabilise as a united, multi-ethnic state is formed - or be further riven, strengthening the tendency to withdraw and reaffirm distinct ethnic boundaries. Guyana's destiny will in fact depend upon the manner in which political and economic power is linked to categorical identities and aspects of a system of meaning in specification of cultural standards and their legitimisation in everyday practices.8 The complex condensation of political and economic power into accepted discourses about Guyanese ethnic identity appears to be of crucial importance in the ongoing evaluation of valid criteria, for evaluating a viable and peaceful coexistence between Indians and Africans.

Yet the road to ethnic unity will be fraught with pitfalls. The economic plight of Guyana, the legacy of poverty, debt and inflation, and the reduction of world markets for Guyana's basic agricultural and mineral produce, will require extraordinary dexterity for any government to remain focussed and impartial; and it will be impossible for these issues to be addressed without reopening traditional fears of ethnic domination.

Recent events in Guyana do not seem to point to an amelioration of this vacillating tendency. It is easy to see that any eruptions of bitter ethnic conflict re-invoke the fears which accompanied the very worst excesses of the 1960's. Jagan, when finally restored to office did seem to have a genuine desire to break the cruel wheel of ethnic polarisation which he and his rival Burnham helped to build into national consciousness. As David Hinds (who was President in 1997) suggested, in an article a few years ago, Guyana has developed such irreconcilable ethnic rivalries constantly relied upon and manipulated after independence. The struggle for power became a zero sum game between two iconic leaders:

"Dey needed one another to be what dey became. You tek dat from me. Burnham frighten black people wid Jagan jumbie, an Jagan frighten Indian people wid Burnham jumbie.[9] In de end Guyana become a jumbie country. Boy, both a dem deform we, dat today none ah we can see pass we nose. Dats why Guyana gone fuh Channa." (David Hinds, Saxakali 1997)

The political climate I have detailed, one of anxiety and stalemate, post-election violence, allegations of non-judicial police executions, torture and mistreatment of suspects[10] does not point to a country that has put these ghosts to rest. Whether Jagan allowed the ethnic divisions to operate to his advantage in the early days of the PPP and after the rift within their ranks, it nevertheless seems that he developed a genuine desire to find a solution that would resolve the polarised state and share power more effectively between all groups.

'while Dr. Jagan lived, a lid was placed on open ethnic insurgency. His message of "racial/class/ideological balance", "inclusion and partnership" and national reconciliation was neutralising broader sectors of the society.' [11]

Furthermore Jagan's attempt to take a global view of the social, political and economic predicament of Guyana and other developing nations became increasingly apparent before his death. In a speech to the United Nations he made the point that "Colonialism is certainly not extinct and today threatens to survive in different forms. Many aspects of colonialism are evident in the ever widening gap between the developed and developing countries and in the dependence of impoverished millions on the largesse of a few."

This is certainly a key issue in Guyana's plight, yet one wonders if the most pernicious affects of colonialism are those which do not present themselves directly to economic analysis, they are the internalized and durable dispositions (habitus) which have been generated by the divisive exploitation of the colonial era and are now imbedded deeply in the institutions and practices of Guyana.

The dream of a peaceful and plentiful multi-ethnic state which Guyana certainly has the potential to become has been deferred. The bitter irony is that the dream of a future untainted by horrors and torn by political and economic rivalry will never be achieved whilst the ethnic divisions create a divided psyche where the dream is one not to be shared.

NOTES AND REFERENCES

1 Williams, B, 1991

2 Williams, B, 1991 , p159

3 Williams, B, 1991, p185.

4 Jenkins, R, 1992, pp79-97.

5 See Muecke, S.1982

6 Williams B. F., 1991, pp253-254.

7 ibid

8 ibid

9 jumbie – a ghost or spirit,

10 http://web.amnesty.org/web/ar2002.nsf/amr/guyana?Open Amnesty International Publications 2002

11 http://www.dreamwater.org/jahajis/Moses.html

12 Jagan, 1997: 477 (from the new Epilogue 3)

BIBLIOGRAPHY

Agee, P (1975), Inside the Company: CIA Diary, Penguin: London
Alexander, V, Guyanese Culture Through Prism of Race and Class, University of Guyana Symposium.
Amnesty International: http://web.amnesty.org/web/ar2002.nsf/amr/guyana?Open
Banton, M.P (1967), Race Relations, Tavistock: London.
Banton, M (1983), Racial & Ethnic Competition, Cambridge University Press, Cambridge.
Bartels, D (1978), Class conflict and Racist Ideology in the Formation of Modern Guyanese Society, PhD Thesis, University of Alberta.
Bartels, D (1981) 'Catastrophe Theory and Dialectical Change in Guyanese Race and Class Relations', Current Anthropology Vol 22, No.4, August 1981.
Barth, F, (1969), Ethnic Groups & Boundaries, Norway.
Barthes, R, (1973) Mythologies, Paladin.
Bassier, D (1980), Kali Mai Worship in Guyana: A quest for a new identity, WMZ,
Bentley, G. Carter, (1987) Ethnicity & Practice, Comparative Studies in Sociology & History, No. 29
Bhagwan, M (1966), Riot Commission Report Examined, Education & Research Committee, People's Progressive Party, New Guiana Co.
Bourdieu, P (1989), Distinction: A Social Critique of the Judgement of Taste, Routledge.
Bourdieu, P (1990) In Other Words, Essays toward a reflective Sociology, Oxford Polity Press.
Bourdieu, P (1977), Outline of Theory of Practice, Cambridge University Press.
Bourdieu, P (1989), The Logic of Practice, Cambridge Polity Press.
Braithwaite, L (1974), Contradictory Omens, Monograph 1, from a public address in Mona, Trinidad, 1974.
Brass P.R. (1985), Ethnic Groups & the State, Croom Helm.
Brereton, B (1974), 'The Foundations of Prejudice, Indians & Africans in Nineteenth Century Trinidad', Caribbean Issues, Vol 11, No. l, 1974.
Burnham, F (1970), Destiny to Mould, Harlow, Longman.
Burnham, J (1964), Beware My Brother Burnham, New Guiana
Carter, M (1966), 'A Question of Self Contempt' in M. Carter and G. Lamming (eds.), New World Magazine.
Chase, A (1964), A History of Trade Unionism in Guyana 1900-1961, Ruimveldt, Guyana: New Guyana.
Cohen, R (1978) 'Ethnicity: Problem & focus in Anthropology', Annual Review of Anthropology, Vol 7
Cross, M (1972), The East Indians of Guyana & Trinidad, London, Minority Rights Group.
Curtis, M (2003) Web of Deceit, Vintage.
Dabydeen, D (ed) (1995) Cheddi Jagan: Selected Speeches 1992-1994, Hansib
Dabydeen D. (1988) Coolie Odyssey, Hansib
Dabydeen D & Samaroo B (1987), India in the Caribbean, Hansib/University of Warwick.
Daly V (1974) The Making of Guyana, London, Macmillan.
Despres, L (1967), Cultural Pluralism and Nationalist Politics in British Guiana, Chicago, Rand McNally & Co.
Despres, L (1975), 'Toward a theory of ethnic phenomena', in Leo Despres (ed.)
Dening G (1992) Mr. Bligh's Bad Language, Cambridge University Press

Ethnicity and Resource Competition in Plural Societies, The Hague: Mouton & Co, USA.

Douglas, M (ed.) (1975) Implicit Meanings, London, Routledge & Kegan Paul.

Enloe, C (1980), Ethnic Soldiers, University of Georgia Press.

Garnham, N, & Williams, R (1980), 'Pierre Bourdieu and the Sociology of Culture', Media, Culture and Society, 297-312.

Gibson, Kean (2004) The Cycle of Racial Oppression in Guyana

Glasgow, R A (1975), Guyana: Race & Politics among Africans & Indians, The Hague, Martinus Nijhoff.

Goffman, E (1959) The Presentation of the Self in Everyday Life, Garden City, N.Y., Doubleday.

Goffman, E (1981) 'On Face Work : An Analysis of Ritual Elements in Social Interaction', in B. Blount (ed) Language, Culture & Society.

Gopal, M (1982), Politics, Race, and Youth in Guyana, Mellen Research University Press, San Fransisco.

Greene J E (1974), Race vs Politics in Guyana, Mona Inst.of Social & Economic Research.

Guyana Chronicle Online (2005) Archives for April 04 2005 [Online document] http://www.guyanachronicle.com/ARCHIVES/archive%2004-04-05.html (Accessed on 20/1/2006)

Guyana Human Rights Association (1989 & 1990), Guyana Human Rights Report, Georgetown, Guyana.

Guyana Under Siege – online docs - Guyanaundersiege.com, Declassified Documents on British Guiana ht©2001-2003. Government Information Agency (GINA).

Haraksingh, K (1974), 'Review Article', Caribbean Issues, Vol 11, 1974.

Harker, R et al (ed) (1990) An Introduction to the Work of Pierre Bourdieu, Macmillan.

Hintzen P, & Premdas, R (1987), 'Guyana: Coercion and Control in Political Change', Journal of Inter-American Studies & World Affairs, Vol.24, No3.

Hintzen, P (1989), The Cost of Regime Survival: Racial Mobilization,Elite Domination, and Control of the State in Guyana and Trinidad, Cambridge University Press.

Hope, K. R (1985), Guyana: politics and development in an emergent socialist state, Mosaic Press.

Jagan, C. (1998) (ed. by Dabydeen, D) The USA in South America & other essays, Hansib

Jagan, C. (1998) 3rd Edition Forbidden Freedom,Hansib

Jagan, C (1997), The West on Trial, Hansib.

Jayawardena, C (1963), Conflict & Solidarity in a Guianese Plantation, London, Athlone Press.

Jeffrey H B, & Baber C (1986), Guyana: Politics, Economics & Society,Beyond the Burnham Era, Francis Pinter, London.

Jenkins, R (1992), Pierre Bourdieu, Routledge.

Janes, H (1981), Crime Race and Culture, Chichester, Wiley.

Kissoon, F (1991) 'Cricket, racialism and Guyana's future' in Catholic Standard, 31 March, 1991

Kissoon, F (1991) on harassment of Indian-Guyanese market traders in Catholic Standard, 31 March, 1991

Kissoon, F (1991) Article about attitudes to the elections - in Catholic Standard, April 21, 1991

Kwayana, E (1988), More than Survival: Afro-Guyanese and the Nation, University of

Guyana Commemoration Commission.

Laguerre, J G (1987), Pluralism & the Guyanese Intelligentsia', Caribbean Quarterly, Vol 33.

Landis J B (1971), Race Relations and Politics in Guyana, Unpublished doctoral dissertation.

Latin America Bureau (1984), Guyana: Fraudulent Revolution, London: Latin America & The World Council of Churches.

Mandle J R (1973), The Plantation Economy :Population and Economic Change in Guyana, 1838 - 1960, Temple University Press.

Manley, R (1979), Guyana Emergent, Schenkman Publishing Co.

Mars, P (1990), 'Ethnic Conflict & Political Control: The Guyana Case', in Social & Economic Studies, Vol 39.

McGowan, Winston (1989), The African Slave Trade to Guyana, Guyana Historical Journal.

Milne R S (1981), Politics in Ethnically Bipolar States, UBC Press.

Moore B (1987), Race Power & Social segmentation In Colonial Society 1838-91, New York, Gordon & Breach Science Publisher.

Muecke, S (1982), Available Discourses on Aborigines, Theoretical Strategies.

Naipaul, S (1981), Black & White, Abacus.

Nath, D (1970), The History of Indians in British Guiana, D. Nath, London

Newman, P (1964), British Guiana: Problems of Cohesion in an Immigrant Society, Oxford University Press.

Premdas, R (1972), 'Elections & Political campaigns in a Racially Bifurcated State: Guyana', Journal of InterAmerican Studies.

Premdas R (1972b), Voluntary Associations & Political Parties in a Racially Fragmented State, Georgetown: University of Guyana.

Premdas, R (1974), 'Guyana: Communal Conflict, Socialism and Political Reconciliation', Inter-American Economic Affairs, Vol.30.

Premdas, R (1978), 'Guyana: Socialist Reconstruction or Political Opportunism ?', Journal of Inter-American Studies & World Affairs, Vol.20.

Premdas, R (1981), 'Guyana: Violence & Democracy in a Communal State', Plural Societies, Vol 12.

Premdas, R (1986), 'Politics of Preference in The Case of Guyana' in Kennedy et al (eds), Ethnic Preference & Public Policy in Developing States.

Premdas, R (1987), Political Power, Race and Human Rights in the Caribbean: The Guyana Case.

Premdas, R (1992), 'Ethnic & Racial Conflict in the Caribbean' in B. Samaroo and C. Debidin (eds), Ethnicity & Indians in the Caribbean, Macmillan, London.

Rabushka, A, and Shepsle (1972), K, Politics in Plural Societies: A Theory of Democratic Instability, Charles E Merrill.

Ramesh, D (1987), 'The Social Psychology of Cultural Pluralism', Caribbean Quarterly, Vol 33.

Rauf, M (1974) An Indian Village in Guyana, a study of cultural change & ethnic identity, Leiden, Brill.

Rodney, W (1981), A History of the Guyanese Working People, 1881-1905, Baltimore, John Hopkins University Press.

Rodney, W (ed) (1979), Guyanese Sugar Plantations in the Late Nineteenth Century, The Argosy, Georgetown, Guyana, Release Publishers.

Rose, J (1989), 'The Repatriation Controversy & the Beginning of an East Indian Village System', Guyana Historical Journal, Vol 1.

Ryan, S (1972), Race & Nationalism in Trinidad & Tobago: A study of decolonisation in a multiracial society, University of Toronto Press.

Sanders, A (1987), The Powerless People, Warwick University Caribbean Studies.

SBS World Guide (1992), Melbourne Text Publishing.

Shepherd, V (1988), Indians and Blacks in Jamaica in the Nineteenth and Early Twentieth Centuries: A Micro-Study of the Foundations of Race Antagonisms, Frank Cass.

Simms, P (1966), Trouble in Guyana: an account of people, personalities and politics as they were in British Guiana.

Singer, P (1967), 'Caste and Identity in Guyana' in B.M. Schwarz (ed), Caste in Overseas Indian Communities, San Francisco, Chandler.

Singh, C (1988), Guyana: Politics in a Plantation Society, N.Y., Praeger, Stanford University.

Skinner, E. P (1955), 'Group Dynamics & Social Stratification In Guyana', Annals of the New York Academy of Sciences, no. 83.

Smith, M G (1974), The Plural Society in the British West Indies, University of California Press, London.

Smith, R T (1962), British Guiana, London, Oxford University Press.

Smith R T (1965), The Negro Family In British Guiana. Family Structure &Social Status in the Villages, London: Routledge & Kegan Paul.

Spencer, S (2006) Race and Ethnicity: Culture, Identity and Representation, Routledge.

Spinner, T (1984)., A Political & Social History of Guyana, 1945-1983, Westview.

Stabroek News (2001) 'Racial Divide Must be Bridged Now' 30th September, 2001

(2002) on racially motivated killings, Nov 5th, 2002

(2003) On stalemate between ruling party and opposition, April 4th, 2003

Sukdeo, I D (1982), The Emergence of a Multiracial Society of Guyana, New York.

Sunday Times, Nov 5, 1968, p4

Sunday Times, April 16 & 23, 1967

Thomas, C (1982), From Colony to State Capitalism: Alternative Paths of Development in the Caribbean, Faculty of Social Sciences & Institute of Development Studies, University of Guyana.

Thomas, Clive (1984), Plantations, Peasants, and State: A study of the Mode of Sugar Production in Guyana, 1984, CAAS Monograph Series 5, Los Angeles Center for Afro-American Studies & University of California Press.

Turpin, Tim (1990) The Social Construction of Immigrant & Aboriginal Ethnic Group Boundaries in Australia, PhD thesis, La Trobe University

Vasil, R K (1984), Politics in Bi-Racial Societies: The Third World Experience, New Delhi, Vikas.

Vincent, J (1974), 'Brief Communications', Anthropology, Vol.33.

Walks, H A (1979), Neo-Colonialism & Social Relations In a PostColonial Society: Guyana 1966-74, Thesis.

Williams, B F (1991), Stains on My Name; War in My Veins, Durham, Duke University Press.

Young, C (1976), The Politics of Cultural Pluralism, University of Wisconsin Press.

Zizeck, S (1990), 'Eastern Europe's Republics of Gilead', New Left Review.

WEBSITES FOR FURTHER RESEARCH

http://www.gina.gov.gy/archive/releases/gr030806.html
Guyana needs new strategic vision and focused leadership
http://www.dreamwater.org/jahajis/Moses.html
ORGANIZED CRIME, A MOST SINISTER KIND OF CRIME THAT IS HUGE AND

GROWING Part 2 Prem Misir, Ph.D.
On the Hermandston Accord see:
http://www.eabguyana.org.gy/Elections2001/HerdmanstonAccord.htm
On the St Lucia Summit: http://hostings.diplomacy.edu/iirt/chronology/Update9o.htm
http://www.sdnp.org.gy/mininfo/archive/researchp/rporganisecrime.html
for interesting and comprehensive bibliography try
http://www.mbeaw.org/resources/countries/guyana.html
http://www.newint.org/issue310/profile.htm
http://guyana.gwebworks.com/synopsis.shtml#Demographics

INTERVIEWS

Martin Carter, Georgetown, April 1991
Kusha Haraksingh: 18.3.1991
Dr Dennis Bassier: University of Guyana: 11.4.1991
Dr Cheddi Jagan : Freedom House: 4.5.1991
Eusi Kwayana: WPA HQ: 21.4.1991
Louis (Afro-Guyanese surveyor) Buxton 11/4/91
Griff (former police chief) & Leonard Arokium – Demenico House Recorded in Georgetown, 5/3/1991
East Indian bus conductor -Georgetown 13 April 1991.
David Decaries: Stabroek News offices: 3.4.1991
Prof Clive Thomas: University of Guyana: 3.4.1991
Brim Pollard - CARICOM n Georgetown 2 April 1994.
Nigel Westmaus: WPA HQ: 9.4.1991

Appendix 1

Despres' Multi-dimensional ethnic identity

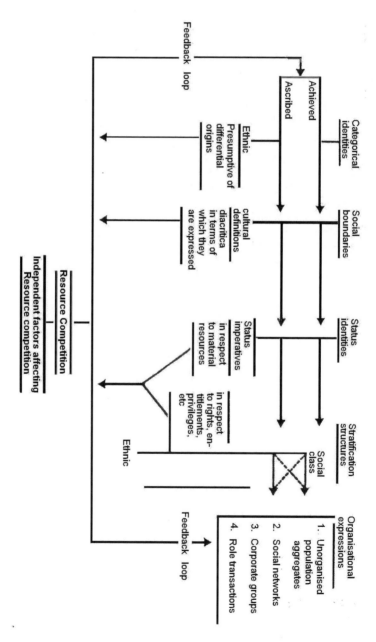

Fig. 1. Framework for the comparative study of ethnic phenomena adapted from - Leo Despres (1975) *Towards a Theory of Ethnic Phenomena*

Appendix 2

Hierarchy of Givers and Takers
(adapted from Williams, B, 1991: 166)

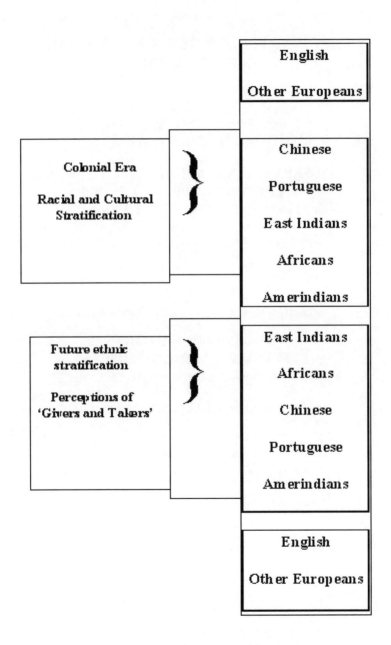

Appendix 3

People's Coalition for Democracy handbill (1991)

PCD ANTI - HUNGER & FREE & FAIR ELECTIONS CAMPAIGN

DLM, NDP, PPP, TUF, URP, WPA
Join forces to keep hunger away

DEFEND THE PEOPLE'S RIGHT TO EAT

OBSERVE A NATIONAL DAY OF REST
TUESDAY. APRIL 9'TH, 1991
FROM DAWN TO DUSK

MAKE TUESDAY A DAY OF NON-COOPERATION WITH
STARVATION !
EMPTY BAGS CANNOT STAND!
LET THE SYSTEM CARRY ITSELF ON TUESDAY!
Unions are bargaining for their members.
PCD supports all active unions.
WE THE PEOPLE MUST SHOW DETERMINATION
in this simple way

REST DOWN HOME
TUESDAY, APRIL 9TH, 1991!

The government is liming while people have to buy **rice by half-gallon,**
sugar by quarter-pound and **STARVE**

50% CAN'T WUK!   1 DAY-PAY = ½ GALLON RICE

CAN'T WUK!

**HAVE MERCY ON THE POOR LOWER & MIDDLE INCOME
PEOPLE AND PENSIONERS.
THE PEOPLE CRY OUT FOR ECONOMIC AND POLITICAL JUSTICE!
PCD SAYS: REGISTER WITH THE ENUMERATOR !
TAKE BACK YOUR RIGHT TO VOTE !
MINI-BUS & TAXI-DRIVERS! STAY OFF THE ROADS !
JOIN THE PROTEST TO BRING DOWN GAS PRICES..'**

Index